WADSWORTH PHILOSO

ON
BRENTANO

Victor Velarde-Mayol
University of South Florida

Australia • Canada • Mexico • Singapore • Spain
United Kingdom • United States

To Isabel

COPYRIGHT © 2000 Wadsworth, a division of Thomson Learning, Inc. Thomson Learning™ is a trademark used herein under license.

ALL RIGHTS RESERVED. No part of this work covered by the copyright hereon may be reproduced or used in any form or by any means—graphic, electronic, or mechanical, including photocopying, recording, taping, Web distribution, or information storage and retrieval systems—without the written permission of the publisher.

Printed in the United States of America
1 2 3 4 5 6 7 03 02 01 00 99

For permission to use material from this text, contact us:
Web: http://www.thomsonrights.com
Fax: 1-800-730-2215
Phone: 1-800-730-2214

For more information, contact:
Wadsworth/Thomson Learning, Inc.
10 Davis Drive
Belmont, CA 94002-3098
USA
http://www.wadsworth.com

ISBN: 0-534-57611-7

Contents

Preface	1
Chapter 1: Biography and Philosophical Project	2
1. Biography	2
2. Brentano's Notion of Philosophy as a Scientific Discipline	8
3. The Four Phases of History of Philosophy and the Place for a Scientific Philosophy	11
Endnotes	12
Chapter 2: Philosophical Psychology	13
1. Introduction	13
2. Psychology as an Empirical Science	14
2.1. Two Definitions of Psychology	14
2.2. Physical and Psychical Phenomenon	16
2.3. Psychology as the Science of Psychical Phenomena	19
3. Descriptive Psychology	21
3.1. The Notion of a Descriptive Psychology	22
3.2. The Necessary and Universal Laws in Descriptive Psychology	24
3.3 Anti-Psychologism of Brentano's Philosophy	25
4. Nature of a Psychical Phenomenon and its Difference from Physical Phenomenon	27
5. Presentation and Phenomenon	27
6. The Notion of Intentionality	29
7. The Conscious Character of Al Psychical Phenomena, Inner Perception, or Inner Inner Consciousness	33
7.1. Inner Perception	34
7.2. The Unity of Consciousness	37
8. Classification of Psychical Phenomena	41
Endones	42
Chapter 3: Theory of Knowledge	45
1. The Theory of Judgment	46

2. Theory of Terms	52
3. Truth and Evidence	53
4. Analytic and *A Priori* Judgments	58
Endnotes	59
Chapter 4: Metaphysics	60
1. The Fourfold Distinction of Being	60
2. Reism	63
3. The Notion of Being	66
4. Metaphysics of Accident	67
5. Metaphysics of Substance	71
6. Metaphysics of Relation: the Intentional Relation	74
7. Metaphysics of God	76
Endnotes	78
Chapter 5: Ethics	80
1. The Scope of Ethics	80
2. The Freedom of the Will	80
3. The Basic Ethical Principle	81
4. The Concept of Intrinsic Good	84
Endnotes	89
Bibliography	91
1. Selected Bibliography of Brentano's Published Writings	91
2. Selected Bibliography of Brentano's Works	92

Preface

Brentano is one of the most quoted and least studied philosophers. Almost everyone in current philosophy of mind is talking about Brentano's thesis (his doctrine about the intentionality of mental acts), but only a few have studied Brentano's philosophy. As a matter of fact, there are hardly any overviews of the complete philosophy of Brentano in English. Probably this is due to the fact that Brentano's works were translated into English too late. The translations made by Terrell, Rancurello, McAlister, Chisholm, Schneewind, George, Müller, etc., seemed to have arrived when the peak of the interest in Brentano's philosophy decreased considerably. Although Brentano's philosophy is the foundation of Husserl's phenomenology and the whole phenomenological movement, Brentano did not receive the attention Husserl did and still enjoys in our days. Although some of Brentano's theses are the core of current philosophy of mind, there are only a few studies about Brentano's philosophy in comparison with the overwhelming literature in current philosophy of mind. The present book tries to cover this gap and to encourage new scholars in the study of Brentano's philosophy.

Brentano is in the crossroads between the two major philosophical traditions in Western philosophy, namely, Continental and Analytic philosophy. He resurrected the notion of intentionality, which was pervasively used by both philosophical traditions with very different outcomes and applications. In Continental philosophy, phenomenology is a development of Brentano's ideas on intentionality, in such a way, that without this, phenomenology would be impossible. In Analytic philosophy, one of the few notions shared with Continental philosophy is precisely the intentional character of mental acts, but with different application and interpretation. Here, in this book, we will dedicate to Brentano's psychology more attention than to other topics, not only because of its historical influence but also because it plays an essential role in his whole philosophy.

There are some subjects that are missing here: aesthetics and the relations between philosophy and religion. The reason of this lack is only the constraints of space. A decision was made in favor of some topics over others that could illustrate better Brentano's philosophy.

Spring 1999
Rutgers University

I
Biography and Philosophical Project

1. Biography

Franz Brentano was born on January 16, 1838, in Marienberg (Germany). The name of Brentano was well known among German Catholic intellectual families: Franz was the son of Christian Brentano, an important writer, the nephew of the romantic writers Clemens Brentano and his sister Bettina von Armin. Franz's grandfather, Maximilienne de la Roche, is believed to have literary connections with Goethe.

Brentano attended the Royal Bavarian Gymnasium in Ashaffenburg. At the age of seventeen, the last years of his time at the Gymnasium (High School), Brentano remembered having had his first religious doubts, which continued to increase during the rest of his life. During 1855-6, he attended the Lyceum to take the required courses of general education before entering the university, and by 1856 he was already a student of the University of Munich.

During this first period of Brentano's life, he kept a close relationship with his mother, who was a person with deep religious faith and great intellectual abilities; a combination that undoubtedly had a strong impact on the young Brentano. Probably, under the influence of his mother, Brentano became interested in theological issues, and specifically, Aquinas's theology. This interest would survive throughout his life despite his future problems with the Catholic church.

While attending the University of Munich, Brentano went to Berlin (1858-9) to work under the well-known Aristotelian philosopher, Trendelenburg. During this time Brentano read and studied Aristotle in depth, later (1859-60) at the Academy in Münster, he enhanced his knowledge of Aristotelism with the study of the medieval Aristotelians. Brentano demonstrated an interest in Aristotle that endured until the last years of his life. At the age of twenty-four (1862) Brentano published his first book *"On the Several Senses of Being in Aristotle,"* which is a brilliant interpretation of Aristotle's Metaphysics. The book is dedicated to his master Trendelenburg, who considered it one of the most important interpretations of Aristotle's philosophy. Later, in the

Biography and Philosophical Project

same year, Brentano received his doctorate from the University of Tübingen.

He moved to Munich to study theology, but his mind was more inclined for philosophy and natural science. Having finished his theological studies, Brentano was ordained as a priest in 1864. Two years later he habilitated as a *Privatdozen* in philosophy at the University of Würzburg, where he presented a paper to the Faculty on the topic "Exposition and Critique of Schelling's Teaching in his Three Phases," a subject very remote from Brentano's philosophical interests, which makes one suspect that he did not choose it himself. His habilitation thesis was "*The Psychology of Aristotle, in Particular his Doctrine of Nous Poietikos*" published in 1867. Here Brentano tried a different way of interpreting Aristotle, he recommended that the reader become completely immersed in both the spirit of the philosopher and the characteristic thought-patterns of the philosopher being studied. Brentano proposed that to experience the initial conditions of the philosopher being studied it could be very illuminating to reconstruct his philosophical system as if one were the philosopher under study. Thus, Brentano became an authority in Aristotle's philosophy, something that caused very positive commentaries among his colleagues and strong disputes with other interpreters of Aristotle. The Dean, for example, claimed that of all the works that had been submitted to the Faculty of Arts and Sciences of the University of Würzburg in the course of a half century this was definitely the most outstanding one.

Brentano's work on Aristotle is not isolated from the rest of his work. The influence of Aristotle in Brentano's philosophy was enormous, although other philosophical traditions are the starting point of many of his ideas (medieval philosophy, Descartes, Leibniz, British empiricism, and to a lessen extent, Kant), but Aristotle has a privileged place. This can be difficult to understand if we take into consideration that authority is not a reason to follow a philosophical doctrine. Certainly, Brentano used to say that authority could not overcome reason in philosophy, but authority could be a starting point that should be analyzed before being accepted or rejected. This attitude, of course, was valid for Aristotle's authority as well, even although Brentano used to say that Aristotle's ideas were so well crafted and profound that he granted them a certain *prima facie* probability, a certain right to be heard, but at the same time they should be analyze to be accepted or rejected. Brentano's interest and admiration for Aristotle was constant during his life, but this did not mean that he agreed with Aristotle in the same way all his life. His disagreement was increasing to the degree that somebody could think that there is little of Aristotle's philosophy in Brentano's last production. In some way, one would say

Biography and Philosophical Project

that Brentano started as an Aristotelian, and ended up being just an outstanding commentator of Aristotle.

Starting in 1866, Brentano lectured metaphysics, logic, psychology, and history of philosophy. He had a strong influence on his students as is attested by the words and facts of disciples such as Carl Stumpf, Anton Marty, among others. Stumpf, for example, abandoned his studies of law to devote himself completely to philosophy just because of the overwhelming influence of the professor Brentano. Stumpf himself recognized the power that Brentano exercised over susceptible students like himself. A very long list of other disciples underwent a radical metamorphosis of ideas by Brentano.

As a professor, Brentano dedicated much time to preparing his lectures, which were very well structured with strong logical support. He was willing to interrupt long discourses in his lectures just to make concise syllogistic summaries of complicated ideas. Stumpf remembered that during his student years with Brentano, when some students disagreed with Brentano based on vague feelings, simple dislike, or some unhappiness with a certain thesis, Brentano's reply was that it really did not matter whether one was happy or not [1].

Brentano began to teach the history of philosophy in a new way based on his theory of the four stages of philosophy, in which the history of philosophy and the philosophy of history of philosophy became melded in an ingenious hermeneutic principle. He matured his theory of the four phases of philosophy about 1867-9, but its origins can be traced to 1860. Brentano at that time was meditating on how the birth and sudden death of great philosophical systems was possible, specifically the significance of the systems of speculative philosophy in the 19th Century, which was so widely admired for a time and later wholly rejected. Brentano thought that there might be some reason for this based on the intrinsic structure of the history of philosophy regardless of the truth of these philosophical systems. This reason in question may be explained with his theory of the four main periods or phases of the history of philosophy. It is obvious, for any philosopher with some knowledge of 19th Century philosophy, that Brentano's theory of four phases of philosophy is based on and resembles the theory of the three phases of human development exposed by the brilliant and controversial French philosopher, Auguste Comte, founder of modern sociology. Brentano recognized this influence in his published treatise "Auguste Comte and the Positive Philosophy," a paper criticized and rejected by the mainstream German philosophy of that time. Brentano believed that Comte was a realist, but a critical one, in opposing the dominant philosophy in Germany, represented by what Brentano qualifies as the decadent speculative mysticism of the philosophy of

Biography and Philosophical Project

Schelling and Hegel, which overshadowed Comte's ideas. Brentano saw in Comte an idea constantly present in Brentanian philosophy, that is, the idea of a scientific philosophy based on experience, which explains Brentano's dislike for thinkers such as Kant and the post-Kantian German Idealists, whom he considered unscientific. From here, Brentano tried to spread the idea of a positive treatment of philosophy, where the term "positive" is not what the Circle of Vienna later would call "positivism," but rather what Comte meant by "positive," and what Brentano liked to call scientific philosophy.

Brentano's inner break with the Catholic Church came in 1870 after having written a paper against the dogma of papal infallibility. In this paper, Brentano argued that the infallibility doctrine contradicts three major sources —the Gospels, the teaching of the Church fathers, and the complete history of the Church. But it was almost three years before Brentano broke completely with the Church publicly. Definitely, in the same year 1873, Brentano left the priesthood, resigned from his professorship, and abandoned all ties with the Church and Christianity in general. The reader might suspect that Brentano's inner break with the Church was followed by an approach to Protestant faith, but according to Brentano's influential disciple, Husserl, Protestant ideas played no role in Brentano's abandonment of the Catholic faith. His disciple, Stumpf, recalled that Brentano's motives were more of a theoretical nature than of an emotional nature, because he found increasing logical and metaphysical difficulties posed by the mysteries of the Catholic faith [2]. Nevertheless, it is very unlikely that only theoretical motives were at play, and it is more reasonable to think that personal and moral motives were involved at the same time. It is difficult to know what really happened, but the fact that all his life Brentano continued to both preserve a high esteem for the Church and a dislike for any institutional religion indicates an internal conflict and a painful experience which started in his earlier years.

In the meantime, Brentano was studying English, and harboring the idea of going to England to meet the most influential persons and thinkers in the English speaking world. He traveled to England primarily to meet the British philosopher John Stuart Mill — a visit that would not be realized due to the fact that Mill was on a trip abroad. He also planned to visit John Newman, the spirited leader of the English Catholics, but there are no records that a meeting ever took place. Apparently, Brentano first met Spencer in England (1872) and later maintained a correspondence with him. Meanwhile, during his absence from Germany, Brentano was made *extraordinarius* professor of philosophy at the University of Würzburg. Unfortunately, Brentano never met Mill. After writing a long letter to Mill discussing the theory of

Biography and Philosophical Project

knowledge, Mill invited Brentano to meet visit him in Avignon, France, but, Mill died before the two philosophers could meet.

The year following his tumultuous rupture with the Church was one of the most important periods of Brentano's career, he finally was appointed to the University of Vienna as professor *ordinarius* (1874) by the Austrian Minister and, in the same year, published his most famous and important work, *Psychology From an Empirical Starting Point.*" This work created the reputation Brentano enjoys until now, and made him the influential philosopher who is responsible for several philosophical movements in 20th Century Philosophy.

Brentano enjoyed many influential disciples throughout his philosophical career. Some of them were both disciples and friends such as Carl Stumpf and Anton Marty, who followed Brentano even in his tumultuous and tortuous life and religious positions. Other disciples became founders of philosophical schools, such as Edmund Husserl (founder of phenomenology), Alexius Meinong (School of Graz). Others became influential professors in their field, such as Alois Höfler, Kasimir Twardowski, Franz Hillebrand, Christian von Ehrenfelds, among many others. Some disciples were influential politicians such as T.G. Masaryk and von Hertling, who later became opponents during the First World War — von Hertling became the chancellor of Germany, and Masaryk became the first postwar president of Czechoslovakia. Many others were second generation disciples, like Martin Heidegger, whose reading of Brentano's *On the Several Senses of Being in Aristotle* deeply changed his philosophical life, and was the seed for his most important philosophical work, *Being and Time.* Bertrand Russell considered Brentano to be the most interesting philosopher in the European Continent. In addition, Brentano maintained personal exchange of ideas with Ernst Mach, W. Dilthey, and Boltzmann, among others.

A few words about the founder of Phenomenology can be illuminating about Brentano's influence. Husserl attended Brentano's lectures for a short time —only two years only (1884-1885). Husserl held a PhD in mathematics with a minor in philosophy, although things would change after the encounter with Brentano. Husserl recalled that he went to Brentano's lectures at first merely out of curiosity, to hear the man who was the subject of so much talk in Vienna at that time [3], but later he was captivated by the way Brentano treated philosophical problems and decided to become a full-time philosopher.

Brentano's personality at this time appeared very glamorous to everybody. He had a peculiar appearance, attractive philosophical personality, solemnity in his speech, and at the same time, he managed to keep a special glitter and charm [4]. He practiced many extraphilosophi-

Biography and Philosophical Project

cal activities, he was an excellent chess player (he invented a new chess defense still in use today), he had artistic inclinations such as poetry (there is an unpublished volume of Brentano's poetry) and music.

Brentano married Ida Lieben in 1880, but the Austrian Supreme Court did not recognize the marriage of former priests. So, to avoid this problem, Brentano decided to take Saxon citizenship, and married Lieben in a civil court, in order to avoid tensions with the Austrian government. But the problems for Brentano were just beginning. Because of the close ties between the University of Vienna and the Austrian government, which was very concerned with the influence of the Church, Brentano was persuaded to resigned his professorship, which he did under the firm promise by the Austrian government that he would be reappointed as soon as possible. This reappointment never came though.

In 1881, Brentano obtained only a *Privatdozent* at the University of Vienna with the hope that this would be a step toward recovering his professorship, but the Austrian government rejected all recommendations of the faculty of the University and ignored his unprecedented success both among students as a teacher and among his colleagues as a researcher. Tired and feeling defeated, Brentano began harboring the idea of abandoning Austria, a decision that would be materialized some years later.

About 1893, his wife Ida died leaving behind a five year old child. And to add insult to injury, the faculty of the University of Vienna again recommended Brentano very strongly to the Austrian Minister of Education, but this, for political reasons and unfairly, considered that Brentano's case had expired after more than ten years. Later, probably based on the same grounds as other governmental denials was the rejection of Brentano's proposal to create a laboratory for experimental psychology. Nevertheless, Brentano's philosophical activity did not fade but rather became even more intense, and his genius was even better known among the philosophical community.

After too much unfair treatment during more than twenty years of academic service, in 1895, Brentano decided to abandon Austria for Italy. After 1895, he no longer held an academic position; nevertheless, by correspondence, conversation and publications he continued to work at the development of a truly scientific philosophy and its defense against dogmatic speculative constructions that were in fashion in his time. The next year he presented a brilliant paper, "On the Individuation, Quality and Intensity of Sense Phenomena," to the Third International Congress of Psychology held in Munich, 1896. One year later, Brentano married Emile Rueprecht in 1897.

During the following years, Brentano's creativity was very rich.

Biography and Philosophical Project

Among his many works, it is worthy to mention the presentation of an important paper, "On the Psychological Analysis of Sound Quality and its Elements," to the Psychology Congress in Rome, 1905. He also wrote another treatise on Aristotle, *Aristotle and his World Conception* (1911). In the same year, he wrote the book "On the Classification of the Psychic Phenomena," which is an essential expansion of his major work in *Psychology*.

Brentano's last years were not peaceful either. He was left almost blind after several unsuccessful eye operations, and he had to move again and to abandon Florence and established residence in Zurich due to the political situation of Italy, which declared war entering into the World War I. In 1916 he had a severe attack of appendicitis, from which he never recovered. Brentano died on March 17, 1917.

2. Brentano's Notion of Philosophy as a Scientific Discipline

The source of Brentano's philosophy is complex, especially because it is a mixture of both modernization of old doctrines and a highly creative mind, which produced new ideas difficult to trace in the history of philosophy. Nevertheless, one can say —without too much danger of simplification— that Brentano's philosophy is driven mainly by three traditions —Aristotelian philosophy, Medieval philosophy and, Cartesian philosophy. What Brentano carried out in his philosophy is the modernization of classic notions in Aristotle and Medieval philosophy with a strong influence from the Cartesian *cogito*. So, his philosophy is essentially realist with an aversion to any kind of idealism and transcendentalism. But he added to these different traditions the idea that the renewal of philosophy must pass through a scientific method, that is to say, the renewal of philosophy should be to find the scientific path of philosophy in a similar way as other disciplines found this path. Brentano's idea of a scientific philosophy will survive in current American philosophy of mind.

There were many different and contradictory interpretations of Brentano's philosophy, here I will mention only a few of them in order to establish what I would like to do here.

1. There were interpretations of Brentano as an idealist, or a structural idealist,[5] just because his notion of intentional object seemed to create a gap between the extramental thing and the intentional object. But this seems to be a misunderstanding of what intentional object meant for Brentano as we will see later

2. From phenomenological positions such as Husserl's, Brentano's philosophy was considered dangerously close to psychologism, if it were not already a sophisticated form of psychologism. This is

Biography and Philosophical Project

very inaccurate because (i) Brentano always fought psychologism, and (ii) Husserl interpreted Brentano's theory of the mental act to fulfill his own philosophical problems, which do not fit into Brentano's.

3. Husserl and many phenomenologists accused Brentano of naturalizing the consciousness. And this is very likely correct, but the way Brentano saw the naturalization of consciousness is probably very different from the way Husserl did if we take into consideration that Brentano distinguished two types of nature, one for the material world and other for the subject of the mental acts in a way parallel to Aristotle. On the contrary, the notion of naturalization in Husserl is rather a reaction against physicalism. In this sense, it is not appropriate to accuse Brentano of naturalizing mind just as it is inappropriate to say that Aristotle naturalizes the mind.

4. There were attempts to show that Brentano's philosophy was strongly influenced by Kantian Transcendental philosophy. This interpretation seems forced, although it is possible to see some Kantian influence on some issues such as on the unity of consciousness. Nevertheless, this is suspicious because Brentano was almost always viscerally against any form of Kantianism and German Idealism.

It may be that the best way to understand Brentano's philosophy is by distinguishing the different periods of its development and the source of this development. We can delineate at least three periods in his philosophy, which in chronological order are the following:

(1) The Aristotelian period, which starts with his training under Trendelemburg, 1858, with its peak in 1864-66, and does not end although it is fading little by little. The Aristotelism of the last years of Brentano's philosophy is more as a commentator of the Greek philosopher than as his follower.

(2) The Cartesian period, which starts approximately in 1869, with its peak in 1874 when he published his major work, *Psychology from an empirical Point of View*, and ends with the rejection of *irrealia* and fictitious objects (1911).

(3) The critical linguistic period, which starts around 1911 (maybe 1905) and continues until the end of Brentano's life. This period coincides with what was called by Brentanian scholars "reistic period," in which Brentano only accepts things as objects of mind, but things are not only material things because the soul is, for Brentano, a real thing, but not material.

This division of his thought has to be taken *cum grano salis* because there are obvious overlapping periods and enhancements of some subjects of one period into another period that complicate the process of his thought. The following scheme can illustrate this idea:

Biography and Philosophical Project

```
       Aristotelian period
       ━━━━━━━━━━━━━━━━━━━━━━━━━━━━━━━━━━
              Cartesian period
              ━━━━━━━━━━━━━━━━━━━━━━ - - - - - - -
                   Linguistic period
                   ━━━━━━━━━━━━━━━━━━━━━━━━━━
       1869-1874                      1917
   I      I        I                     I
  1858         1905-1911
```

(1) *Aristotelian period.* Brentano states an important principle for his whole philosophy: "the true method of philosophy is none other than that of the natural sciences." In other words, the task of philosophy and empirical science cannot and should not be pursued in separation. With this principle, Brentano tries to reestablish the unity of scientific knowledge that was disrupted with the distinction between the sciences of nature and the sciences of the spirit established by German Idealism. This principle will play an essential role from the beginning to the end of his philosophical activity, and will survive in other philosophical traditions such as Analytic Philosophy.

This Brentanian principle certainly has deep roots in Aristotle; nevertheless there is a caveat because Brentano seems to have in mind two types of science which are put together in some way. (a) Modern science, characterized by a systematic knowledge, based on experience, tested by experimentation, under a hypothetical-inductive method, and oriented to control nature, that is to say, oriented to technology. This notion of science is not Aristotelian. (b) Aristotelian science, which has the features of being a theoretical knowledge, based on experience, with certainty, and for its own sake regardless of practical outcome. Although both notions of science coincide in being based on experience, the Aristotelian science does not use a hypothetical-inductive method but instead uses the method of abstraction from experience. I think that this idea plays an important role in Brentano, although it is not always as explicit as one would like.

When Brentano says that the method of philosophy is the same as the method of natural science, he has in mind that philosophy has to start from experience, and the rejection of *a priori* knowledge. Nevertheless, the modern hypothetical-deductive method is not contemplated by Brentano.

(2) *Cartesian period.* Brentano mixed Aristotelian elements with the Cartesian *cogito*. This can be seen in a second principle of Brentano's philosophy: description of phenomena is prior to their explanation, [6] that is to say, pure description of what happens in the scope of our mind is prior to an exposition of causes of mental processes. This principle has strong connections with the Cartesian

Biography and Philosophical Project

idea that we have absolute evidence of the existence of the "*cogito ergo sum*" and uncertainty about the external world. Brentano modifies this idea by saying that we can reach the highest evidence by describing the psychical phenomenon instead of the casual relations which produced these phenomena and the causal relations in the world. As we will see, this was the origin of his descriptive or phenomenological psychology. On the contrary, for Aristotle there is not such a separation because, in his theory of the four causes, explanation implies description. One, familiar with Aristotle, knows that formalities belong to formal cause, which, in turn, belongs to the order of explanation. In addition to this, Aristotle considered descriptions as an imperfect definition when we do not know the essence of a thing, but in all definitions the four causes are involved in some way or another.

(3) *Linguistic period.* About 1905, Brentano underwent a radical change in his philosophy, which was influenced by his disciple Marty's analysis of language. Both Brentano's development of a scientific philosophy and his attacks against mysterious entities, which are not things but supposedly have being such as universals, abstract entities, ideal objects, and in general unreal objects were carried out by a critique of language (*Sprachkritik*), a sort of linguistic analysis with important metaphysical consequences. The metaphysical position of this period is called "Reism," the doctrine that states that only things can exist and can be objects of thought. A correct linguistic analysis would show that universals, ideal entities, and so on, are only convenient fictions of language and not metaphysical entities.

To this period belong his works published after his death by his disciples from his lectures and put together in *True and Evident, The Theory of Categories,* and *The Rejection of the non-real.*

3. The Four Phases of History of Philosophy and the Place for a Scientific Philosophy

History of philosophy is usually studied in three periods: ancient, medieval, and modern. Brentano's approach to these periods is by discerning four differentiated phases. First: investigation; second: application; third: skepticism; and fourth: mysticism 7.

(1) The phase of investigation is characterized by a general interest in theoretical questions for their own sake, regardless of practical applications. Here, the method is borrowed from the natural sciences.

(2) The phase of application is the beginning of the decline. Interest in theoretical questions diminishes in favor of practical research such as ethics. Philosophical growth becomes slow, and the reach of philosophical questions is more superficial because there is an interest in popularizing philosophy, and the deep theoretical questions are

Biography and Philosophical Project

abandoned as impractical and unproductive.

(3) The phase of skepticism is the natural outcome of the second phase. Brentano thinks that this period could not last too long because skepticism goes against human nature, it is unappealing for most humans, unsatisfying.

(4) The phase of mysticism is a reaction against the phase of skepticism. But this reaction is not a resurrection of philosophy but its most extreme degree of philosophical decay. There is no argumentation but dogma, there is no use of the natural method of the first phase, but mystical intuitions instead.

During the ancient period, pre-Socratic philosophers until Aristotle belong to the first phase, and the last phase of mysticism belongs to the Neo-Platonism of Plotinus. In the modern period, the most fruitful phase of investigation belongs to philosophers such as Bacon until Locke and Leibniz. The second phase of practical applications belongs to the philosophers of the Enlightenment. The third phase of skepticism is represented by Hume. Finally, the fourth phase of mysticism is represented by Kant, post-Kantian idealism, especially, Hegel.

The dominant philosophy of Brentano's time was German Idealism, which he characterized as the most decadent philosophy, and he proposed to replace it by a philosophy that would go back to the first phase, a philosophy based on the scientific method, the method of natural science. Obviously, philosophers such as Aristotle, Locke, Leibniz, etc., who belong to the first phase of the history of philosophy, the most creative and scientific period, were Brentano's heroes.

Endnotes

[1] Carl Stumpf, "Reminiscences of Franz Brentano", in *The Philosophy of Franz Brentano*, Linda L. McAlister (ed.), p. 11-16.
[2] Carl Stumpf, "Reminiscences of Franz Brentano", p. 23.
[3] Edmund Husserl, "Reminiscences of Franz Brentano", in *The Philosophy of Brentano*, p. 47-49.
[4] See Oscar Kraus, "Biographical Sketch of Franz Brentano", in *The Philosophy of Franz Brentano*, p.6.
[5] Cf. Gustav Bergman, *Realism. A Critique of Brentano and Meinong*, Milwaukee, Madison, 1967.
[6] Cfr. Barry Smith, *Austrian Philosophy, the Legacy of Franz Brentano*, p30.
[7] Cf. Franz Brentano, *Die Vier Phasen der Philosophie und ihr augenblichklicher Stand*, edition by Oskar Kraus, Leipzig, 1970.

2
Philosophical Psychology

1. Introduction

Most of the material of Brentano's philosophical psychology is found in his main published work *Psychology from an Empirical Standpoint* (1874)[1], composed of two books. Brentano originally planned six books, but the other four were never written. Book one deals with psychology as a science, and book two is dedicated to mental phenomena and their classification. According to Brentano's plan, the third book would have investigated the characteristics of, and the laws of presentations; the fourth book would have dealt with the characteristics and laws of judgments; the fifth book was supposed to concern itself with emotions and the acts of will; finally, the sixth book was planned to cover the relationship between mind and body. Brentano's psychological investigation is concerned with both genetic and descriptive psychology (genetic psychology has to do with the causal laws of mental activity, and descriptive psychology is just a description of mental phenomena), only later will Brentano distinguished both methods. His general goal was to find the unity of both object and method of psychology as a science.

It is important to take into account that the starting point of Brentano's philosophical psychology is Aristotle, with a strong influence from Cartesian philosophy. This is in sharp confrontation with the psychology of his time, especially against Wundt's psychology. The project of Brentano's psychology is framed in what I will call "philosophical psychology from an empirical point of view" versus Wundt's empirico-deductive psychology. In the lectures on Metaphysics, Brentano uses the term "philosophical psychology" as a part of theoretical philosophy or metaphysics, whose object is the being as such and the human spirit[2]. Therefore, Brentano's psychology is in many ways closely related to metaphysics, and this is especially true in relation to subjects in which the soul is involved, which is latent in Brentano's conception of psychology regardless of his methodological attempts to separate metaphysics from psychology, as we will see below.

2. Psychology as an Empirical Science

2.1. Two Definitions of Psychology

The first objective of Brentano's psychology is to define psychology and its method, which is no different from the method of the natural sciences, *viz.* to start from experience. Looking back on the history of psychology, one discovers a lack of success of psychology as a science. Brentano believed that this problematic lack of success was due —among other things— to the fact that psychology did not take the successful path of the empirical sciences. And the reason that psychology did not become an empirical science was due to the lack of maturity of more basic sciences that are fundamental for psychology.

Brentano conceives of science as a hierarchical body of particular sciences in which each higher step is erected on the foundation of the one below it. A higher science investigates more complex phenomena, a lower one investigates phenomena that are simpler, but which contribute to the complexity of the higher science. The progress of a science that stands higher in the hierarchy presupposes both the development of the lower sciences, and enough empirical evidence. Psychology is a discipline of higher order that needs other sciences of lower order (especially physiology) as its foundation, that is, psychology will flourishes when the whole body of natural sciences is mature enough. In this sense psychology is a science that is the "crowning pinnacle" of the whole body of sciences. Therefore, psychology's failure to achieve the status of science was due to both the fact that the other lower sciences (here, natural sciences) were not well developed and to weak empirical evidence. In the history of science we observe that only when mathematics was developed enough, could physics shine as a science, and this was the foundation for chemistry, and this, in turn, is the basis for physiology, which attained the status of science in the 19th Century. Since mental acts are the most complex phenomena that an empirical science can study,[3] it seems obvious that only when the basic sciences arrive to a sufficient degree of development that psychology can flourish by becoming an empirical science.

Brentano proposes two possible valid definitions of psychology. One is classic in the Aristotelian tradition, and the other has its influence in John Stuart Mill, but it is developed in a different way from Mill's.

(1) *First Definition of Psychology*. For Aristotle, psychology meant the science of soul. Here soul means the first act of a living being, the subject of other activities (second acts) such as nourishing,

Philosophical Psychology

perceiving, understanding, and so on; or more technically, the soul is the substantial form of an organized body. We know that something is living if it self-moves in the sense that it nourishes itself, perceives by itself, and so on, but not only local movement. Aristotle considered vegetative activities as part of psychology as well, but later on, the subject-matter of psychology was narrowed down to conscious living beings. Parallel to this reduction of the scope of psychology, the term "soul" was narrowed just to the bearer of mental activity. Brentano appropriates the Aristotelian notion of psychology with slight modifications: psychology is "the science which studies the properties and laws of the soul, which we discover within ourselves directly by means of inner perception, and which we infer, by analogy, to exist in others."[4] Thus, psychology is an empirical science because is based on experience —inner perception.

It seems that psychology and natural sciences exhaust all possibilities of the area of empirical science (physics, chemistry, biology, etc.). Brentano considers the possibility of a discipline that is between both —the case of psychophysics. Fechner called psychophysics a branch of science in which physical and mental properties form a functional unity. He observed that the facts which the physiologist investigates and those which the psychologist considers are very often intimately correlated. From the fact that physical states are aroused by mental states, and mental states, in turn, are aroused by physical states, Fechner tried to find regularities and laws that connect physiology with psychology. Fechner formulated the laws of these connections, which he called psychophysical laws. Thus, he proposed a new science between physiology and psychology that seems to dilute the great divide between natural science and psychology.

Brentano recognizes the value of psychophysical laws, but believes that they are not capable of justifying a third empirical science in addition to the natural sciences and psychology. A psychophysical law implies two parts, one belongs to physiology and the other to psychology, there is no medium. Brentano's argument is very insightful, and it runs as follows: (a) Physiologists determine the differences in the intensity of physical stimuli which correspond to the smallest noticeable differences in intensity of mental phenomena. (b) Psychologists will register the relations which these smallest noticeable differences bear to one another. (c) Now, it is evident *a priori* that all noticeable differences are equally noticeable (to notice does not admit degrees, either one notices having an experience or one doesn't as we will see later in this chapter). (d) But this does not mean that they have to be really equal as Fechner's psychophysical law assumes[5]. So, Fechner's psychophysical law is not sufficiently established to justify the birth of

15

a third science between psychology and physiology.

(2) *The second definition of psychology.* Another valid possibility to define psychology has to do with the suspension of the metaphysical element of the former definition. The aforementioned Aristotelian definition of psychology has at least two elements —metaphysical and descriptive. The metaphysical element is the existence of the soul, and the descriptive element is the manifestation of the properties and laws of the mental life. Many psychologists will be at odds with the metaphysical element —the existence of the soul— but they will agree with a definition of psychology as the science of the psychical phenomena. The elimination of metaphysical elements from psychology has the advantage of not being committed to entities of which some have serious doubts about their existence. Of course, to be fair with this methodology, a parallel procedure should be expected with natural sciences, which instead of dealing with bodies they now should be defined as the science of physical phenomena. The notion of body —as much as the notion of soul— is a metaphysical consideration, while the notion of physical phenomenon —as much as psychical phenomenon— is neutral. In this sense, both psychology and the natural sciences fall under the notion of phenomenon —psychical and physical— and both are empirical because they are based on experience — inner perception and external perception respectively.

2.2 Physical and Psychical Phenomenon

What is a phenomenon in Brentano's parlance? The term "Phenomenon" means the appearance of some thing. For example, a color is a phenomenon of a thing, a sound is another phenomenon of a thing. A thing is not a phenomenon and a phenomenon is not a thing, but a phenomenon is a manifestation of a thing. A thing becomes a phenomenon for our consciousness when that thing becomes an object of knowledge; a completely unknown thing is not a phenomenon for consciousness. We can know only two kinds of phenomena, those provided by our external perception and those provided by our inner perception, and thus, we have physical phenomena and psychical phenomena, respectively.

(1) *Physical phenomenon* is the appearance of a thing to our external perception, for example, a color, a figure, a sound which is heard, warmth which is sensed. In addition to this, Brentano considers a physical phenomenon to be that which appears to the imagination as well; because a color, a figure, a sound, and warmth can be presented in my imagination. In this sense, imagination forms part of the complex

Philosophical Psychology

process called "external perception." It is important to stress that a horse, a tree, this table, are not physical phenomena for Brentano. Physical phenomena are only the sense impressions of these things, or better, the sense appearances of these extramental things, *viz.* the color, shape, and so on, of a horse, a tree, etc.

Following John Locke, Brentano believes that phenomena like color, sound, warmth, taste, etc., are merely phenomena (sense impressions), they do not really and truly exist outside of our sensations, even though they refer to things which do exist. Nevertheless, physical phenomena in general "are signs of something real, which, through its causal activity, produces presentations of them."[6] (An extramental thing causes a psychical presentation, a mental act, which presents a phenomenon of this extramental thing.) Brentano cites several experiments to prove the non-reality of physical phenomena. (a) Locke's experiment. If one hand was warm and the other cold, and we immerse them in the same basin of water, we will feel warm water with one hand, and cold water with the other. But the same basin of water cannot be warm and cold at the same time; therefore, the sensation of warmth and cold are not real but merely phenomena of our senses. (b) The pressure on the eye can arouse the same visual phenomena as would be caused by rays emanating from a colored thing.[7] In these cases, Brentano believes that colors, sounds, tactile sensations, and so on, are *merely* phenomena (they do not exist outside the mind, they are not extramental). However, because phenomena are signs of something, they have some foundation in reality, but this does not mean that the thing signified by the phenomenon is exactly as the phenomenon prescribes. Obviously, this position leads us to the Cartesian thesis that objects of sensory experience do not guarantee the truth of the existence of external things, they are not fully evident. The interesting conclusion Brentano draws here is that physical phenomena are just that, phenomena and not the thing as such. What we *observe* when we look at the external world are physical phenomena, which are the subject-matter of natural science.

From here, Brentano claims that physical phenomena are not adequate representations of the reality that they signify, and they give us knowledge of reality in a very incomplete sense; therefore, they do not guarantee the truth of the external reality.

(2) *Psychical phenomenon* is the object of inner perception. For example, hearing, seeing, sensing, imagining, thinking, and so on. Brentano uses the expressions "psychical phenomenon," "mental act," "experience," "mental phenomenon," etc., as synonymous. Although psychical phenomena are phenomena, they have important differences

Philosophical Psychology

from the other class of phenomena (physical phenomena). (a) Contrary to the physical phenomenon grasped in external perception, a psychical phenomenon is more than a phenomenon; it is at the same time the reality of a mental act, or psychical act. Psychical phenomena are acts of thinking, acts of hearing, and so on, while physical phenomena never are acts nor activities nor existing things but only the appearance of these things. In other words, while physical phenomena are only phenomena, psychical phenomena are both at the same time, *viz.* phenomena and reality. (b) The reason why (a) is that case has to be found in the difference between external and inner perception. Inner perception provides an immediate insight to the existence of the reality that appears as a phenomenon, we grasp the true reality that the psychical phenomenon signifies. That mental acts are immediately perceived in their reality means that *as they appear to be, so they are in reality,*[8] something that does not happen with physical phenomena. "No one can really doubt that a mental state which he perceives in himself exists, and that it exists just as he perceives it."[9] Mental phenomena are more intimately accessible to us than the physical world; we are living in them, such that not knowing of the existence of our own mental life is like not knowing that we are living.

Several remarks have to be made in relation to the introspection of mental acts. (a) Brentano is talking about *inner perception* of our own mental acts and not *observation* of them. Usually when a psychologists is talking about introspection, he is referring to inner observation of our own mental states. But this is not what Brentano has in mind. Observation requires the presence of *another* psychical phenomenon to present the psychical phenomenon which has to be observed. This distinction is extremely important, as we will see later. (b) Certainly, the object of empirical knowledge falls under either physical phenomena or psychical phenomena, but the way of accessing each phenomena is completely different. The only access to physical phenomena is through observation by means of external perception, that is to say, *a psychical phenomenon is necessary to present the physical phenomenon.* The only access to psychical phenomenon is through inner perception, which means that another psychical phenomenon is *not* necessary to present the psychical phenomenon one wants to perceive. This distinction marks the difference between natural sciences (based on observation), and psychology (based on inner perception). (c) We are absolutely certain of the existence of our mental states through inner perception, but we do not have the same degree of certainty of the existence of physical things through external perception. Our *mental phenomena are the things which are most our own*; they enjoy a special relationship to us that physical phenomena do not.

Philosophical Psychology

While we are having a mental phenomenon we are perceiving it directly at the same time. We can say that *to present a psychical phenomena we only need one single psychical phenomenon which presents itself; on the contrary, to present a physical phenomena we need two phenomena, the psychical phenomenon (or mental act) that presents the physical phenomenon and the physical phenomenon itself.*

2.3. Psychology as the Science of Psychical Phenomena

Regardless of the Cartesian impact on Brentano, his Aristotelism plays a more important role in his psychology. This is obvious when he states that both external and inner perception exhibit substances to us. Through inner perception we apprehend ourselves as the subject (substance) of our mental states (the soul as the subject of perceiving, remembering, thinking), or better, we have an infallible perception of ourselves as psychologically active.[10] Through external perception we apprehend something as the subject (substance) of qualities (i.e., things are the subject of extensions). To assume that there is an attribute or quality without any subject supporting it is logically untenable; nevertheless, Brentano thinks, we can pretend for a while that mental acts and physical qualities are without a subject. Brentano considers that this is a comfortable fiction, that is not only harmless, but useful insofar as it temporarily suspends the judgment of a metaphysical controversy about the existence of the soul. In this sense, it is a methodological position to talk about physical and psychical phenomena instead of material bodies and immaterial substances (souls).

The empirical laws (for example, laws of coexistence and succession) and facts that the traditional conception of natural science as the science of bodies investigates continue to be investigated by natural science when it is conceived restrictively as the science of *physical phenomena*. The same is true about psychology. The phenomena revealed by inner perception are also subject to laws. It means that if a psychologist denies the existence of a subject (soul) of mental states, it also will be true for him that the psychical phenomena are under the same empirical laws (for example, laws of coexistence and succession) as if the psychologist does not deny the existence of the soul.[11]

Brentano recognizes that the British philosopher John Stuart Mill had a similar idea of psychology —psychology investigates the laws which rule the succession of our mental states. For Mill, the task of psychology is to construct the whole mental life from the most elementary laws of mental phenomena, in a similar way as mechanics and chemistry derive complex phenomena from simpler ones. In this sense, Mill's model of psychological analysis is a *chemistry* of mental phenomena. This idea had a strong impact on Brentano, but not without criticism.

Psychology as the science of psychical phenomena can be interpreted in two senses. Brentano rejects the first interpretation and accepts the second one.

(1) *Explicit rejection of the metaphysics of the soul.* Psychology as the science of psychical phenomena can imply an explicit rejection of the existence of a substance or subject (soul) as the bearer of these psychic phenomena. This is Hume's view that there is not a bearer of mental phenomena but a bundle or collection of different phenomena. Although this interpretation of psychology as the science of psychical phenomena takes into account the same laws of psychic phenomena as psychology defined as the science of the soul and its properties, Brentano insists that it leaves an important gap —the question of continued existence after death. Many philosophers will not see this as a problem but as an advantage. It is said that the abandonment of the investigation of the immortality of the soul in psychology is a sign of maturity in this science, a necessary step in reaching the qualification of empirical science. Chemistry, for example, had to abandon alchemy in order to become an empirical science, and similar things have to be said of physics and physiology. Brentano disagrees with this position because the case of psychology is not identical to the natural sciences; psychology is not a natural science, although it uses the same empirical method as natural science. These are the reasons Brentano has in mind: (a) Psychical phenomena are not a subclass of physical phenomena, as we will see below; and (b) in place of alchemy's dreams, reality is a higher substitute, but the laws of association of ideas are a very insufficient substitution for the loss of an investigation of the immortality of the soul. (Brentano makes the observation that it is possible to consider the issue of immortality even though there is a rejection of the substantiality of the soul. In this case, obviously, there will be no immortality of the soul, which is rejected, but immortality of life.)

(2) *The coexistence of both definitions of psychology.* There is nothing in the second definition of psychology —the science of psychic phenomena— that could not be accepted by the first definition of psychology —the science of the soul and its properties. Regardless of the question of the existence of the soul, both definitions of psychology coincide in admitting the existence of mental phenomena. *Whoever accepts the Aristotelian definition of psychology as the science of the soul (first definition) will accept the other definition as the science of psychical phenomena (second definition).* The difference is that the first definition contains metaphysical statements from which the second

Philosophical Psychology

is free and, as a consequence, simplifies the research. To be fair with this methodology, psychology as the science of psychical phenomena should make abstraction not only of the bearer of mental phenomena, but also of other metaphysical assumptions, for example, evolution of mental life from other forms (Brentano agrees with the theory of evolution, but rejects it in the way Darwin proposes it.)

This means that Brentano accepts a definition of psychology as the science of mental phenomena with the possibility of a psychology without a soul, despite his own philosophical certainty of the existence of a spiritual substance that is immortal and the bearer of mental phenomena. This is consistent with Brentano's notion of phenomenon as a sign of what appears, for we can abstract what appears and study only the appearance, but from here one cannot draw the conclusion that there is not some extramental thing that appears.

Both definitions of psychology are empirical and share the same empirical method. And both definitions of psychology have similar sources, which Brentano summarizes in three points. (a) The primary source of an empirical psychology is inner perception, but it is not the only source. (b) A secondary source for an empirical psychology is the inner observation of past experience, that is, our *memory of past experiences*. In this case it is possible to focus attention on the contemplation of our mental experiences in memory. However, as Brentano says, following the Cartesian tradition, the results will not enjoy the evidence of inner perception, but only a probable knowledge based on memory. This fallibility of memory is and has been the origin of mistakes in psychology. (c) Another source of an empirical psychology is the expression of mental states made by others, humans or non-humans.

3. Descriptive Psychology

3.1. The Notion of a Descriptive Psychology

Brentano gave a series of lectures during 1888-1889 at the University of Vienna titled "Descriptive Psychology or Descriptive Phenomenology." Later (1890-1891) he revised his lectures under the title "Psychognosis".[12] Husserl attended the 1888-1889 lectures at the University of Vienna and recognized that without these lectures Phenomenology would not have been possible [13]. And although there are important differences between Brentano's descriptive psychology and Hussserl's phenomenology, Husserl had all the elements to develop his own phenomenology from Brentano's ideas. It is very tempting to go further by saying that phenomenology had its first days in Brentano's

Philosophical Psychology

1888-1889 lectures.

As the expression means, descriptive psychology describes the psychical phenomena of human consciousness. Descriptive psychology is in contrast to genetic psychology, which is concerned with explanations, causal connections of psychical phenomena. Descriptive psychology does not explain any phenomena, it is just an analysis of what is presented to perception, a descriptive analysis of psychical phenomena. Descriptive psychology is related to genetic psychology as anatomy is related to physiology. And because psychical phenomena are present to us directly, without mediation, the truth of our inner perception is without error (psychical phenomena are *incorrigibilia*), but Brentano goes further by claiming that descriptive psychology is an exact science. This means that a description of a psychical phenomenon by inner perception is fully present to us from all sides. On the contrary, because genetic or explanatory psychology is based on induction from our external perception, it cannot be an exact science. (a) First, because genetic psychology is under the fluctuation and unstable veracity of our senses (we sometimes experience that our senses deceive us even in the more familiar things about the world); and (b) secondly, because induction is only a statistical generalization from instances, which cannot guarantee the necessity and universality of an exact science.

Nevertheless, descriptive psychology is not a substitute for but a preliminary step towards genetic psychology, which shares the method of natural sciences, that is to say, genetic psychology is not only empirical but explanatory like natural sciences. In contrast, descriptive psychology is empirical but not explanatory. Brentano's goal is to bring the method of natural sciences into philosophy, but we need an intermediary step to obtain the concepts involved and to establish a solid starting point based on direct evidence; this intermediary step is descriptive psychology.

The main goal of descriptive psychology is to describe the nature of basic psychical phenomenon from which all other psychical phenomena are derived. From the combination of elemental or atomic psychical phenomena it is possible to arrive to complex psychical phenomena, just as the totality of words can be derived from the combination of the totality of letters. This procedure is almost identical to what Leibniz had in mind —and Descartes before Leibniz— about the *characteristica universalis*. Brentano is looking for the *characteristica universalis* of all psychical phenomena as the basic elements to reconstruct complex mental phenomena.

Given this account of descriptive psychology, it is easy to understand why Brentano thinks that this new discipline is the basis of all

Philosophical Psychology

philosophy; without it logic, metaphysics, ethics, and so on, would loose their justification. Brentano puts it in a vivid analogy, without descriptive psychology all other sciences would dry up in a similar way as branches cut off from a tree.[14]

Brentano suggested some rules on how to proceed in descriptive psychology, here I mention some of them: (a) To experience the phenomenon, (b) to learn how to notice that phenomenon, (c) to fix what was noticed in order to collect it or retain it in the set of data, (d) from here, to make inductive generalizations and intuitively to apprehend general laws of these psychical phenomena.[15] All these rules imply an accurate description of the noticed psychical phenomenon.

According to these rules, first of all, one must have the experience that has to be analyzed because a psychical phenomenon can only be properly described within our own subjectivity field. Then one has to learn how to pay attention to the inner perception that all experience enjoys, that is to say, one has to notice that an experience or psychical phenomenon is occurring within one's own subjectivity field. Then, one has to describe what is given by inner perception, and this description will be the basis for making inductive generalization in order to apprehend the general laws that connect one psychical phenomenon with another.

These general laws are, according to Brentano, apodictic and universal, that is, necessary and valid for all cases, and at the same time these laws are scientifically stated, that is to say, empirically grounded. These statements break with almost four centuries of Western philosophy, in which apodictic and universal laws cannot be derived from experience (*a posteriori*) but they have to be *a priori*. Obviously, Brentano's theory raises several questions. How can a pure and simple description of our own particular psychical phenomena yield apodictic and universal laws? And how can these laws be verified by others if the source is inner perception, of which only we have privileged access? Verification is an essential element of science: If a result cannot be verified by others, then it will not enter into the body of scientific knowledge; it will be put aside as an unverified case. We will start with the second question, while the first question will be left for the next section.

Brentano considers the objection posed by the second question inaccurate. We cannot have a direct verification, but it is possible to have an indirect one. (a) We can verify (or reproduce) in ourselves what others report to have perceived internally, in other words, we can repeat in ourselves the type of psychical phenomena that others report. (b) We can have an indirect and only probable knowledge of the psychical phenomena of others when they are expressed mainly by language.

Philosophical Psychology

Proof that this is possible is the fact that an educated person is not at loss to find the necessary words with which to express his mental states and at the same time to be understood.[16]

3.2. The Necessary and Universal Laws in Descriptive Psychology

Brentano claims that apodictic and universal laws of psychology are grasped intuitively by describing psychical phenomena. The next question that we have to answer now is how can a pure and simple description of our own particular psychical phenomena yield apodictic and universal laws? By describing instances of psychical phenomena we arrive at the concepts of these phenomena, whose analysis establishes the necessity, impossibility, or possibility of relating the concept of one phenomenon with the concept of the other phenomenon. In this procedure, one can be helped by ordinary induction to go from particular descriptions of psychical phenomena to the concept under which these particular phenomena fall. Because ordinary induction does not give the necessary conditions, we ultimately have to use intuition, which consists of grasping the concept with the necessary and universal laws *at a single stroke*, so to speak, without relying on induction from any particular case.[17] This means that in apprehending one confirming instance of a law, it is possible to see *ipso facto* —we grasp at a single stroke, intuitively— that the instance falls under a concept. This procedure is not very different from what we find frequently in the following example. By describing particular squares we arrive at the concept of square, and the conceptual analysis of this yields the necessary and universal law that "All squares are rectangles."

What is in question here is the meaning of intuition in this context. The intuition Brentano has in mind is a kind of seeing, to see at a single stroke the category or concept under which a particular instance falls. Obviously, this intuition is not a simple seeing but a categorical seeing, or an eidetic seeing —to pick the necessary and universal conditions of an instance, or to remove the particular conditions of a thing until the type or concept appears before our mind, and under that concept an instance is placed. In an Aristotelian fashion, in which Brentano has to be interpreted, this intuition consists of seeing the *intelligible conditions of a particular instance*.

Now, this intuition is performed without any ordinary induction, but, as Brentano argues, some kind of induction is necessary. Brentano has in mind the following argument to support this kind of induction. (a) Induction is the operation of deriving universal and necessary laws from particular instances. (b) But ordinary induction from instances only can yield a probabilistic knowledge. (c) Now, intuition

Philosophical Psychology

also starts from particular instances of psychical phenomena to establish apodictic and universal laws among these phenomena. (d) Therefore, intuition implies some sort of induction in a broad sense. Because it cannot be an ordinary induction, it will be an *intuitive induction*. It is intuitive because the apodicticity and universality is grasped in one single mental movement (at a single stroke), it is not necessary to see many cases, one could be enough, and it is a sort of induction because it goes from particular instances to general laws,[18] and —we can add— it is categorical or an ideation because it yields apodictic and universal knowledge.[19]

Concepts are based only on intuition, and it is not enough to have empirical knowledge. Concepts are not "automatically" guaranteed to start from experience —famous examples are natural scientists, who felt qualified to do philosophy, but were unable to arrive at universal and necessary conclusions— but we need inductive intuition to yield concepts, from where it is possible to discover necessity and universality.

At this point we discover three kinds of inner knowledge —inner perception, inner observation through memory (the only possible inner observation), and inductive intuition. A question rises spontaneously; how can Brentano justify the generalization of the intuitive induction from an empirical point of view? Is not inductive intuition a source of a priori knowledge à la Husserl, and, therefore, a non-empirical knowledge? Brentano does not need any a priori knowledge such as Kant or Husserl invokes. It is enough for him to recall two points. (a) It is important to see that these apodictic and universal laws have an empirical basis because the intuition of these psychological laws require some experience or other by inner perception. In other words, inner perception is another source of experience such as external perception. In this sense, Brentano is right to call himself an "empiricist"; (b) if we read Brentano's thesis from the perspective of his Aristotelian roots,[20] we do not need to make Brentano's intuitive induction fit into Husserl's intuition of essences (which Brentano explicitly rejects because he considers essences purely and simply fictitious entities). It is enough to see a sort of abstraction from the particular cases provided by inner perception.[21] What is missing in Brentano is the mechanism of abstraction once he explicitly rejected the Aristotelian agent intellect, and this incomplete mechanism of abstraction is what seems to bother some commentators, who try to fit Brentano into one of these two opposite extremes, viz. British empiricists or Husserl's phenomenology.

3.3. Anti-Psychologism of Brentano's Philosophy

Brentano's psychology not only plays a central role in his phi-

Philosophical Psychology

losophy but also it is the source of universal and necessary knowledge, as we saw in his descriptive psychology. Is Brentano's philosophy a form of psychologism? Husserl and Frege define psychologism as the naïve and mistaken attempt to base logical and mathematical laws on psychology. Indeed, this procedure is naïve and mistaken because one cannot derive the necessity and universality of mathematics and logic from contingent and problematic generalizations about the ways in which we happen to think, believe, feel, etc. In other words, induction generalization does not yield necessity and universality, but only a probable knowledge. But as we just saw here, Brentano agrees with this attack to psychologism, and he criticized very sharply the psychologism found in John Stuart Mill, who derives logical laws from the psychological laws of association. Certainly, Brentano escapes from psychologism as far as he rejects (ordinary) induction to derive necessity and universality, and creates a new philosophical tool — (eidetic) intuition— to derive necessity and universality. Psychologism is the mistake of deriving an absolute valid norm from a contingent psychological fact (in this sense, Brentano thinks that positivism and historicism commit the same mistake). One should remember that the British philosopher G.E. Moore was very impressed with Brentano's objections to Mill's psychologism and called the attempt of deriving ethical universal laws from contingent facts the "naturalistic fallacy". A psychologist, Brentano argued before Moore, has to admit how absurd it is to think that a normative science such as criminal law could be derived from psychiatry. Thus, Brentano can be counted among the opponents against naturalism and, in a lesser degree, a return to Kant's positions.[22] However, the rejection of psychologism is not a set back for empiricism either, or better, it is not a set back for grounding psychology on an empirical starting point: (a) As we said before, Brentano is called an empiricist because inner perception is a source of empirical knowledge, and (b) Brentano thinks that the method of the natural sciences is the only correct one, and, ultimately, the goal of descriptive psychology.

The discovery of descriptive psychology is also the recognition of the limited applicability of the (ordinary) inductive method of natural sciences, which cannot provide the foundation for the universal and necessary laws of logic and mathematics. This is the reason Brentano later (1889) considered descriptive psychology an autonomous science.

In conclusion, Brentano's notion of descriptive psychology does not allow us to see a return to psychologism. (a) The way inner perception and inductive intuition are interacting makes a radical difference from other psychologies based on introspection (observation). (b) Brentano's distinction between genetic or explicative psychology and

Philosophical Psychology

descriptive psychology is a radical differentiation between the psychologist conception of psychology and the psychologism-free psychology respectively.

4. Nature of a Psychical Phenomenon and its Difference from Physical Phenomenon

The first task of a descriptive psychology is the distinction between a psychical phenomenon and a physical phenomenon. Brentano finds these differentiating characteristics in at least three points: (a) Psychical phenomena are characterized negatively as unextended, while physical phenomena can be extended or unextended; (b) all psychical phenomena are characterized positively by the mark of intentionality, something which is not found among physical phenomena; (c) all psychical phenomena are consciousness of themselves, something which is not a characteristic of any physical phenomena.

We will address the first characteristic now, and we will leave the other two for the next sections.

Brentano agrees with the Cartesian tradition that psychical phenomena have the special characteristic of being unextended, while physical phenomena can be extended or unextended. For example, a color always appears with some extension and spatial location (we see colors on the surface, which has a place); but psychical phenomena like thinking, desiring, and the like appear without extension and without location. However, many physical phenomena appear without extension, especially with respect to sounds and olfactory phenomena which lack the feature of extension. Although, contrary to Brentano's opinion, he recognizes that some important philosophers do not agree with the idea of the lack of extension of all psychical phenomena. Aristotle, for example, whom Brentano follows on many issues, stated that sense perception is the act of a bodily organ, but Brentano thinks that Aristotle stated this thesis without any proof.[23] Because of these opposing opinions voiced by important philosophers, Brentano thinks that this criterion of separation between psychical and physical phenomena is not adequate, and assuming that it were, it would be only a negative criterion to characterize psychical phenomena —non-extensibility— and negative criteria are not sufficient as logical criteria to characterize something. Negative characterization implies a positive one, hence, Brentano prefers to look for positive properties of psychical phenomena.

5. Presentation and Phenomenon

The notion of phenomenon implies the notion of presentation of a

Philosophical Psychology

phenomenon. So, before describing what is a presentation, let us improve the description of a phenomenon.

As it was stated above, the subject-matter of descriptive psychology is psychical phenomena; and a phenomenon is an appearance, but *an appearance of some thing to some one*, there are no appearances of some thing without a subject who receives the appearance. Phenomena are not restricted to sense-impressions. Phenomena encompass physical phenomena, which are sense-impressions for Brentano, and psychical phenomena, which are not sense-impressions. In Brentano's notion of phenomenon, there is an imbalance in the way a physical and a psychical phenomenon are characterized. Physical phenomena are sense-impressions, such as a color, a sound, etc., and these are not real. The color red of an apple is simply an affection of our optical receptors. On the contrary, a psychical phenomenon is the mental act itself, the real thinking, the real judging, etc. Here, the phenomenon is a reality present to me in inner perception. Brentano goes further when he states that we can derive the idea of self from the inner perception of a psychical phenomenon, and we can derive the idea of substance from any impression or perception whatever. This is due to the nature of the phenomenon as such which is a sign of something.

Now we may introduce the notion of presentation, which will be the first important thesis of Brentano's psychology:

Thesis-1   The presentation or the act of presentation is different from the object of presentation.[24]

A presentation [25] is the act that grasps (presents) an object, for example, the act of hearing presents a sound as the object of the phenomenon of hearing, the act of seeing presents a color as the object, and in general, all acts of presentation present an object that is different from the very presentation. This thesis is very important because it is a departure from empiricist psychologies such as Hume's, for whom sense-impressions are confused with the act of sensing. For example, in the presentation of hearing a sound, the sound should not be confused with the psychical act of hearing. In the presentation of seeing a color, the color should not be confused with the psychical act of seeing.

The notion of presentation implies the notion of the object presented, and this is what Brentano called a phenomenon. In this, the presentation is always different from the phenomenon which is presented —the presentation of a color red is neither red nor colored, the presentation of a sound is no sound at all, the thought of fire (a hot phenomenon) does not burn, and so on. This feature is not found

Philosophical Psychology

among any physical phenomenon. In addition, without this thesis the rest of Brentano's psychology would not work.

The notion of presentation leads us to the second thesis of Brentano's psychology:

> Thesis-2   All psychical phenomena are presentations or are grounded in presentations.

This thesis has to be understood in correlation with the first thesis, that is, a psychical phenomenon is an act (a mental act), and presentations are acts (mental acts) and not the objects presented. The second thesis assumes that the set of psychical phenomena embraces not only acts such as presentations, but also judging, feeling, etc. The second thesis establishes that the phenomenon of presentation is absolutely necessary to have any other psychical phenomenon: *nothing can be judged, desired, etc., if it is not presented before.* For example, one cannot judge that A is B if the objects A and B are not presented by the act of presentation; one cannot desire A if the object A is not presented by the act of presentation.

An important caveat: here, the term "presentation" is not what sometimes in current analytic philosophy of mind and cognitive science is called representation; that is to say, to picture a thing or to have an image of a thing, or just to have an idea of a thing. Presentation for Brentano is purely and simply the most basic mode of appearing before the consciousness. In Brentano's mind, a representation would be just "re-presentation," to present an object again. In this sense, memory and fantasy are re-presentations of what was presented before. Interestingly, Brentano uses the German word *"Vorstellung"* for what here we render as "presentation." In Brentano's parlance *"Vorstellung"* has a similar meaning as the medieval word *"representatio,"* which is sometimes understood as *"rei presentatio,"* which is rendered into English as "presentation of a thing."

In this sense, the pheonomenon of presentation is always presupposed for any other psychical phenomenon or conscious phenomenon.

6. The Notion of Intentionality

The main characteristic of psychical phenomena that distinguishes them from any physical phenomena is their intentional character: "Every psychical phenomenon is characterized by what the philosophers of the Middle Ages called the intentional (or mental) inexistence of an object, and what we might call, though not wholly unambiguously, reference to a content, direction toward an object (which is not to be understood here as meaning a thing), or immanent objectivity."[26] In a

Philosophical Psychology

more succinct description, "Every mental phenomenon includes something as object within itself"[27]. This is the third thesis and one of the most important ones of Brentano's psychology:

> Thesis-3   All mental phenomena have the property of the intentional reference to an object, which is equivalent to immanent objectivity, or intentional inexistence of an object.

We can analyze the thesis of intentionality of psychical phenomenon on three levels or aspects: a psychological aspect (all psychical phenomena are characterized by the property of a reference of intentionality), a gnoseological aspect (all psychical phenomena have a reference to an object which does not need to be a thing), and an ontological aspect (the intentional inexistence of an object).

(1) The psychological aspect establishes that intentionality is an essential property of all psychical phenomena that it is not found in any physical phenomena. That this property is essential means that it cannot be missing in any psychical phenomenon. The property of intentionality is described as the reference to an object, the direction toward an object. For example, when one is thinking of a number, the psychical phenomenon of thinking has the essential property of directing itself to something different than itself, an object. Thus, no physical phenomenon has this property. For example, a color does not refer intentionally to anything; a color has some chromatic properties, brightness, and so on, but it does not refer intentionally to anything. On the contrary, the act of thinking, in addition to being something real in our mind, refers intentionally to something other than the very act of thinking. It refers to a number (if we are thinking of a number). Like the act of thinking, desiring, representing, seeing, hearing, and so on, manifest the same property of intentionality, the direction upon an object. In summary, *all psychical phenomena refer intentionally to an objec, while no physical phenomena have this property.*

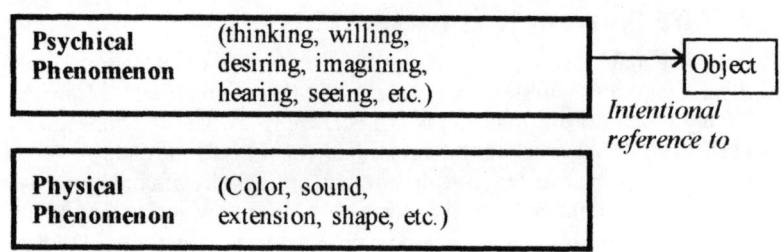

30

Philosophical Psychology

Indeed, Brentano does not give us proof of this mental property because he does not need to, it is a property discovered directly by inner perception, and it is a fundamental datum we perceive internally. When we have an experience of seeing the color red, for example, we perceive that this visual experience carries our attention to the color red, the experience transports us to the object of color red. When one has the visual experience of red, one does not observe the experience itself but the color red, the experience (the mental act, or psychical phenomenon) transports us to the object (here, the color red) intentionally.

To illustrate this point better, let us consider two objections to this influential Brentanian thesis: there are psychical phenomena that seem not to be intentional (for example, feelings), and there are some physical phenomena that seem to be intentional (for example, words).

Feelings (the phenomena of pleasure and pain) seem not to have the property of being intentional because the act of feeling seems to be fused to itself without refering to something different. It seems that feeling pain is just that, pain, but Brentano contends that this is incorrect, and mantains that pain refers to an object; it is intentional as well. One feels pain in the foot, in a hand, in the stomach; sometimes it is vague, but there is always an object different from the psychical phenomenon of pain. Of course, it is not necessary that the object of a psychical phenomenon is an external object, it can be internal. For example, the pleasure of hearing a sound, the object of pleasure is not the sound but the mental act of hearing the sound, we are pleased by having the experience rather than of the sound.[28]

Words have meaning, so they can refer to something different from the physical materiality of the word. They are signs of something else. The word "table" means or refers intentionally to a physical table, which is not the physical word "table". Certainly, a word refers to something different than the physical phenomenon of that word, but Brentano would say that words borrow their intentionality (or meaning) from a psychical phenomenon. We need a speaker to use words, and a hearer to grasp the meaning conveyed by the speaker. Without a mind there are not words, without psychical phenomena there is no meaning.

A caveat: in contemporary analytic philosophy and in the philosophy of mind influenced by it, there is the deep belief that intentionality is only a feature of propositional attitudes (a relation between the mental propositional attitude and a proposition, for example, if you believe that there is extraterrestrial life, your propositional attitude of believing has an intentional relation to the proposition "there is extraterrestrial life"), and this idea is believed to come from Brentano. This is very inaccurate because Brentano understood intentionality as a property of every psychical phenomenon such as feelings, imagining, sense experience, and not only propositional attitudes.

(2) The gnoseological aspect of intentionality establishes that the direction upon an object does not have to be the direction upon an individual thing, it can be non-things. Brentano distinguishes between "thing in general" (*Ding*), "individual thing" (*Realität*), "actuality" (*Wirklichkeit*), and existence (*Existenz*). When Brentano says that the object of a psychical phenomenon does not need to be a thing (*Realität*), he means that the object can be an abstract object, such as universals, which are not individual things. Other examples of non-things or abstract objects are species, genera, ethical and aesthetic values, states of affairs, and so on. In addition to this, an individual thing (*Realität*) can be an actual individual thing (like this tree, this table, etc.) or a non-existent individual thing (like Hamlet, Pegasus, and so on). Imaginary objects that do not exist are individual things for Brentano. So, we have that that the object upon which a psychical phenomenon is directed can be either an individual or an abstract object. Because abstract objects do not exist, and individual objects can exist or not; so, we can modify Brentano's statement by saying that a psychical phenomenon refers intentionally to existent or non-existent objects; or in a more technical way, the intentional object does not need to exist. In this sense, we can say, too, that from the mere fact that something is the object of an intentional act, one cannot infer whether it exists or not. Very interestingly, Brentano thinks that this last claim is true only for physical phenomena but —as we saw before— not for psychical phenomena which are necessarily existent (perceived with evidence by inner perception).

(3) The ontological aspect of intentionality reveals that any psychical phenomenon is ontologically characterized by the intentional inexistence. The ontological consideration of intentionality has caused many headaches among contemporary philosophers. This is especially true with regard to the influential American philosopher, Roderick Chisholm,[29] who considered himself a follower of Brentano. Chisholm interpreted the expression "intentional inexistence" as the non-existence of an intentional object. For example, when one is thinking of the Centaur, this object does not exist in reality, but the object is something with intentional non-existence in our mind. This is inaccurate as we will see.

In order to understand what Brentano meant, we have to see the medieval origins of the notion of intentional inexistence. The term "existence" means effective existence, while the term "in-existence"

Philosophical Psychology

does not mean non-existence but *existence-in-the-intention*. In other words, "inexistence" means that the object is placed in (exists in) the intentional direction of a psychical phenomenon. Now, existence in this sense is not effective existence but existence in a very loose sense, as when a mathematician says that *there are* imaginary numbers, although in reality there *are* no such imaginary numbers.

Brentano tries to resolve the problem of these two very different senses of existence in a very brilliant way. He distinguishes between the *modificative* and *determinative* use of a word. For example, in the expression "a wise man," the word "wise" determines the meaning of the word "man" to the class of men who are wise; so, "wise" is here used in a determinative manner. But in the expression "a dead man," the word "dead" *modifies* the meaning of the word "man" to the extent that the word "man" does not mean a real man any more. "Man" means a living human being, while "dead" means something (a corpse) without life, and both words together would be a contradiction in terms (a non-living living being). So, Brentano thinks, "dead" is used here to modify the meaning of the word "man" to indicate a human corpse, which is no longer a man. If we apply this procedure to the word "existence," we will have similar results. In the expression "an existent horse," the word "existent" determines the meaning of the word "horse," but in the expression "the existence in the intention of the object Pegasus" the use of the word existence is modificative. So, "intentional inexistence" does not mean the effective existence-in my mind, but that an object (like Pegasus) is *intentionally possessed* in the psychical phenomenon. In a more technical parlance, intentional inexistence of an object is the *existence intentionally referred to* the object.

7. The Conscious Character of All Psychical Phenomena, Inner Perception, or Inner Consciousness

The fourth thesis of Brentano's psychology, and one of the most important along with the intentional thesis, is the conscious character of all psychical phenomena:

> Thesis-4   All psychical phenomena are conscious of themselves.

This thesis is not only against the idea that there are unconscious mental acts, but this thesis also is the foundation of Brentano's psychology. To understand what Brentano meant with this important thesis, we have to analyze it with the ideas of inner perception and psychi-

Philosophical Psychology

cal phenomenon, and then to analyze it with his thesis of the unity of consciousness.

7.1. Inner Perception

In addition to the property of intentionality, "Another characteristic which all mental phenomena have in common is the fact that they are only perceived in inner consciousness, while in the case of physical phenomena only external perception is possible."[30] What Brentano here calls "inner consciousness" is what he called elsewhere "inner perception" because to perceive internally that one is seeing a color is the same as saying that one is conscious of having an act of seeing a color. This thesis is very important in Brentano's philosophy and it is essentially connected with the intentional character of psychical phenomena. Brentano binds together in a single unity the intentionality of psychical phenomena with their inner perception; in other words, *there is no possibility of intentionality without consciousness of oneself, nor consciousness without intentionality.* The main reason for this is that an unconscious consciousness is a contradiction. If one is conscious of an object, one is *ipso facto* conscious of oneself; we cannot be conscious of a color, for example, and ignore that we are conscious of a color. Another example, if we have an experience (a mental act, a psychical phenomenon) of smelling roses, we will notice that we are having that experience, otherwise we will not be able to tell that we are having an experience of smelling roses.

Thus, the fourth Brentanian thesis can be reformulated in this way:

> Thesis-4a   It is a characteristic of each psychical phenomenon that it can be perceived internally.

Inner perception does not mean that (a) one can perceive our psychical phenomena as the first thing known, and (b) that inner perception can become self-observation. First, Brentano repeatedly says that it is only while our attention is turned toward an object other than the psychical act that we are able to perceive the psychical act or experience which is directed toward the object of attention. That is to say, the first thing known is an external object, and incidentally our own psychical phenomenon. From here we have another variant of Brentano's fourth thesis:

> Thesis-4b   Every psychical phenomenon is only perceived concomitantly when our attention is directed toward an object other than the psychical act.

Philosophical Psychology

This means that the observation of physical phenomena in external perception offers two kinds of knowledge: the very knowledge of the physical phenomenon, and *at the same time*, the attainment of knowledge of the psychical phenomenon. There is no independent knowledge of the psychical phenomena without our attention to the physical phenomenon. When one attends to a physical object, incidentally, one perceives the mental act which is directed toward that physical object. This restriction to inner perception can seem as an obstacle to psychology, but Brentano makes the interesting observation — which was widely explored in Husserl's phenomenology— that we can turn our attention to physical phenomena in our imagination, which will have the same result as paying attention to a physical phenomenon coming from external senses (the phenomenon red perceived has the same quality as the phenomenon red imagined). So, turning to the physical objects of our imagination we can perceive concomitantly or incidentally the very mental act which is directed to that object.[31]

In the last period of Brentano's philosophy, he explained this characteristic in a very illuminating way. An object enters into a thought in each of the two modes: *modo recto* and *modo obliquo*.[32] In *modo recto* we perceive externally a physical phenomenon, and in *modo obliquo* we perceive internally the very mental act directed to that object and only while it is directed to that object. This implies that a psychical act has two objects, the primary object of the intentional reference, perceived in *modo recto*, and the secondary object of the intentional reference, perceived incidentally or concomitantly, or *in modo obliquo*.

Second, once we are perceiving the mental act, this perception cannot become direct inner observation or direct self-observation. Inner perception can never become inner observation because we need to change our attention from the experience one is having. For example, suppose that one wants to observe his own anger raging within him. One has to abandon the attention given to the object of anger in order to direct it to the very experience of anger. But then the anger must already be somewhat diminished, faded, and so the original object of observation would disappear. From here, Brentano concludes that *we can never focus our attention upon the object of inner perception*, although, as we said before, an indirect inner observation is possible through memory, that is to say, we have to memorize the physical phenomena and then to bring the memory to our attention.

Nevertheless, the problem is still more complex. What is the difference between having an experience and being conscious of that experience? Is it possible to have the experience of seeing a red color and not be conscious of having that experience? In other words, can we have the experience of the color red and not notice it? Here, in these questions, the expressions "being conscious of an experience," and "noticing an experience," are equivalent and bear the same meaning as inner perception or inner consciousness. Brentano admits that it is possible to have a confused inner perception, to notice confusedly our own psychical phenomena. One can perceive an object without perceiving *explicitly* its parts, but in order to resolve this problem, Brentano distinguishes between explicit and implicit inner perception. For example, it is a fact that one can hear a chord and not hear the component notes of the chord. This implies —according to Brentano's distinction— that we have an *explicit* inner perception of the experience of the chord, and only an *implicit* inner perception of the experiences of each note of which the chord is composed. This is Brentano's argument:

(1) It is impossible to have the whole without the parts.

(2) So, it is impossible to have the experience of a chord which does not contain the corresponding experiences of each note making up the chord.

(3) Now, it is a fact that there are people who hear a chord who do not know the parts of the chord.

(4) From here we have two possibilities: (a) there are unconscious experiences of the notes that are part of the chord, or (b) there are, in some way, conscious experiences of the notes that are part of the chord.

Brentano thinks that (4.b) can be fully justified if one distinguishes between *explicit* and *implicit* inner perception. In this sense it is possible to notice explicitly the experience of a chord (to perceive internally that one is hearing a chord), and not to notice explicitly the experiences of the notes that are part of the chord. Instead, they are noticed implicitly, and they can become explicit later. A different example can illustrate the interesting problem of implicit inner consciousness. It happens frequently that we are very concentrated reading a book when the door bell rings. Some will not notice (?) (perceive internally) that the experience po of the door bell is ringing, but later we will realize that the door bell rang. Maybe we do not remember how much time elapsed since it rang, but we now know it rang. In this example, Brentano would resolve this puzzle in two ways: (a) we noticed the experience of the sound, but we forgot its occurrence, at least temporarily, and (b), more interestingly here, we noticed explicitly the content of our reading and implicitly the sound of the door bell, which became explicit later.

Now, explicit and implicit inner perception does not mean that inner perception, or noticing, or inner consciousness, has degrees. Inner perception is the source of immediate evidence, and evidence has no degrees —something is evident or it is not (as Descartes and most of the medieval philosophers would agree). Brentano distinguishes between noticing or inner perception and attention. If we are paying attention to the reading of a book, the inner perception or noticing of the experience of reading is explicit, while the inner perception of the sound of the door bell is implicit because our attention is not directed to it. It frequently happens that, while absorbed in some thought, we pay no attention to other experiences we are having, giving the false impression that we are not conscious of those experiences. In other words, one may speak of "attending well," but it is misleading to speak of "noticing well." Inner perception is always present when one has an experience, it is our attention that makes noticing explicit.[33]

So far, Brentano has made important distinctions related to inner consciousness:

(a) Inner perception is (i) noticing our own mental acts; (ii) it is the inner self-consciousness of any psychical phenomenon, and (iii) it is always present with the occurrence of an experience.

(b) Inner perception is not inner observation because the latter requires two psychical experiences while the former demands only one.

(c) The psychical phenomenon is only perceived concomitantly with the perception of an external object. In other words, inner perception occurs when one is having an observation of an external object.

(c) Inner perception can never become direct inner observation because we need to redirect our attention from the experience one is having, with the undesirable result that one is missing the experience that one wants to observe directly.

(d) Inner perception is not attention; inner perception always has the same degree of consciousness, while attention admits various degrees.

(e) The distinction between implicit and explicit inner perception is an effect of our attention because inner perception as such is always present, whether one attends to it or not.

7.2. *The Unity of Consciousness*

An application of the thesis of universal inner perception of all psychical phenomena is the unity of consciousness. There are two issues regarding the unity of consciousness: first, how does one know that the same subject of consciousness persists through temporal change? This question is a particular case from a more general question that Brentano studies in his *Psychology from an Empirical Standpoint*,[34] which is how does one know that the subject of consciousness when one hears and when one sees is the same? I will limit myself to this last question.   Second, we need an account of how time consciousness occurs, how consciousness grasps internal time so that it experiences itself as a unity.

As to the first point, how do I know that I am the same subject that now sees and now hears? How do I know that the subject that now is thinking is the same as the subject that now is desiring, or imagining?

First, it was previously established that the consciousness of the primary object (consciousness in *modo recto*) is the same consciousness of the secondary object (consciousness in *modo obliquo*), both are two aspects of one and the same unitary psychical phenomenon or mental act. But this does not answer our initial question, because it frequently happens that we have a rather large number of objects before our minds simultaneously, and the question remains whether with such a large number of mental phenomena there is still a real unity which holds them together. There are pathological cases —split brain, for example— in which the patient dissociates what happens with one sense from that of the other. The patient does not recognize that what she sees is the same as what she touches. Based on this clinical fact, some philosophers and psychologists think that consciousness is not a unity but a bundle of mental phenomena instead.

To simplify this issue, we will limit ourselves to the following question, how do I know that the one who hears is the same as the one who sees? That is to say, how can we prove that there is a unity of consciousness when we are presenting different primary objects such as sound and color? Brentano argues in the following way. It is a fact that we compare colors that we see with sounds which we hear; this happens every time we recognize that they are different kinds of phenomena. Now, how would this presentation of the difference among phenomena be possible if the presentations of color and sound belonged to different subjects? We have the following ideas that will draw a conclusion.

(1) Should we attribute the unity of consciousness to the presentation of color or to the presentation of sound, or to both of them taken together, or to some third thing?

(2) Obviously, we cannot attribute this unity to the presentation of color nor to the presentation of sound taken separately because each of them excludes one of the two objects which are compared. Nor can we attribute this unity, for the very same reason, to a third reality, unless we admit that the presentations of color and sound are repeated and united in that unity of consciousness.

(3) Should we, therefore, attribute such a presentation to both of

them together?

(4) But anyone can see that this, too, would be a ridiculous hypothesis. In fact, it would be like saying that neither a blind man nor a deaf man could compare colors with sounds, but if one sees and the other hears, the two together can recognize the relationship.

(5) And why does this seem so absurd? Because the cognition which compares them is a real objective unity, but when we combine the acts of the blind man and the deaf man, we always get a mere collective and never a united real thing.

(6) *Conclusion.* Only if sound and color are presented jointly, in one and the same reality, it is conceivable that they can be compared with one another.[35]

Suppose you are playing piano from a score. In order to know that what you are reading in the score is really what you are playing, and what you are playing is what the score sounds like, you must be able to compare what you are reading with what you are performing and hearing. Can you imagine if the subject who reads the score is different from the subject who plays the piano, and both are different from the subject who hears the result of the performance?

Brentano refers to inner perception as the primary source of knowing that there is a subject of all our mental acts, a subject that is the cause of the unity of consciousness. In inner perception I know — Brentano claims— directly and immediately that the subject that sees is the same as the one that hears, and the same as the one that desires, judges, infers, or doubts, etc. There is one individual thing which is the subject of all our experience, and we know this by inner perception, which is a direct presentation of the psychical phenomenon, which is, in turn, a sign of the subject that bears it. On the contrary, natural science does not have this direct knowledge or presentation, because external perception or observation always implies at least two phenomena —psychical and physical— while in inner perception the same psychical act presents itself without mediation.

Some commentators [36] make the observation that Brentano is influenced by Kant on the issue of the unity of consciousness. Although there is some truth in this, the fact is that Brentano always manifested antipathy to Kant and his philosophical deviations —German idealism.

Going beyond the project of a descriptive psychology (in which metaphysical questions are not explicitly considered) to a metaphysical psychology, Brentano is interested in the argument of the existence of the spiritual soul. From the unity of consciousness, Brentano argues for the existence of the spiritual soul. The argument proceeds from the subject of mental phenomena, which is the bearer and the cause of the unity of consciousness, to a required characteristic of this subject: the

Philosophical Psychology

subject of mental phenomena is *nulldimensional*. This property is in opposition to the three dimensional character of physical entities. This implies that a subject with the property of nulldmensionality cannot be physical, that is to say, the soul is essentially different from physical bodies. It is important to stress that the property of nulldimensionality, and not intentionality, is the distinguishing feature of the soul. Brentano very probably arrived at this idea through his study of the *nous poietikos* (agent intellect) in Aristotle.[37]

Regarding our second point, how does consciousness perceive internal time as the time of a unitarian consciousness? Brentano's disciple, Stumpf, remembers in Brentano's lectures an interesting explanation of time consciousness.[38] At every moment of an inner or external perception, a presentation is produced of the content of the perception (a phenomenon) that is qualitatively the same phenomenon but which is temporally more remote. The characteristic of time is a determination of content whose regular alterations are subject to the very laws of consciousness. In reality this process is an original association as opposed to the acquired associations of memory.

If several impressions (I at t_1, I at t_2, I at t_3) follow one after another, we see that at the entrance of the second one the first has already been pushed back in the above-stated manner, and so on. In the following sketch, the horizontal line means the objective passage of time, the vertical lines are the psychological presentations as they exist at each point:

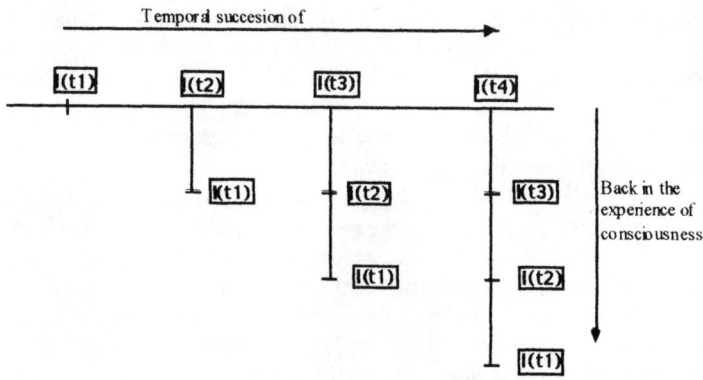

This brief summary of Brentano's theory of time consciousness is a theory about the transformation of content or phenomenon of presentation. Brentano changed his theory later in which the transformation

Philosophical Psychology

was not about the content but the mode of presentation. The reason behind this change was to avoid admitting irrealia such as past objects (the past as past is not real) and only to admit real objects. We will say more about this in the next chapters when we have the opportunity to study his critical-linguistic period or reistic period.

8. Classification of Psychical Phenomena

In order to avoid *a priori* classifications, and consistent with his empirical approach, Brentano follows here the Aristotelian method.[39] Brentano proposes that the classification of psychical phenomena has to be a result of the classification of the objects of these psychical phenomena. This method is based on the principle that the object of a psychical phenomenon specifies the type of the corresponding psychical phenomenon. And in addition to this, a correct scientific classification of psychical phenomena should arrange the objects of psychical phenomena in a manner favorable to research. To this end, it seems natural to unite into a single class objects which are closely related by nature, and separate into different classes objects which are distant by nature. So, the first task in classifying the psychical phenomena is to gather enough knowledge of the objects to be classified.

Brentano justifies this method of proceeding from the object to the type of mental act by stating that "nothing distinguishes mental phenomena from psychical phenomena more than the fact that something is immanent as an object in them".[40] What Brentano calls "immanent object" here is the same as the intentional object, the object upon which a mental act directs itself, or what he also calls intentional inexistence, which means "the existence of an object intentionally referred to." For example, the color red is the intentional object of seeing, and this intentional direction is what, sometimes, Brentano calls immanent object. Therefore, the way of classifying mental acts is by classifying the corresponding intentional objects. Remember, that inner perception only occurs when the psychical act is directed to the primary intentional object; so, a classification of this mental object will lead us to a classification of the psychical phenomena.

Brentano finds three general kinds of mental acts: presentations, judgments, and emotions.[41] Each one corresponds to simple and compound objects (color, sound, white house, etc.), truth and falsity, and good and bad.

Presentation is the basic mental act. As we saw before, a presentation is whenever something appears to our consciousness. For example, when we see something, a color has to be presented; when we hear something, a sound has to be presented; when we imagine something, an image has to be presented. This type of mental act is so basic (see

Philosophical Psychology

Thesis-2 in this Chapter) that "it is impossible for conscious activity to refer in any way to something which is not presented."[42]

An act of judgment is the psychical act that accepts something as true or rejects it as false. For example, "the house is white" is a judgment that expresses the truth if there is a mental act (judgment) that accepts the object white house as true, and expresses the falsity if there is a mental act (judgment) that rejects the object white house as false.

The third class of mental acts is the most difficult to grasp. The psychical acts of emotions are called sometimes "phenomena of interest" or "phenomena of love". In this group we should include the phenomena of pleasure or displeasure, and the phenomena of wish, desire, volition, decision, etc. Brentano sees all these phenomena as belonging to one class "phenomena of emotion or interest".[43] Sometimes, Brentano proposes calling this group "phenomena of love and hate", an expression that is more rooted in the Aristotelian tradition than the word "emotion," which seems to be more rooted in the Humean tradition. A phenomenon of love and hate is characterized by the corresponding object of good and bad. "Just as every judgment takes an object to be true or false, in an analogous way every phenomenon which belongs to this class takes an object to be good or bad."[44] We manifest love, interest, desire, etc. because the object is convenient for us, and a convenient object for us is called "good." We manifest hate, disinterest, aversion, etc. because the object is not convenient for us, and a non-convenient object for us is called "bad."

In addition to this, it is very important to take into consideration, that based on inner perception, we realize the existence of these three types of mental acts, and because the inner perception in all three types is the same (and inner perception is the self-conscious property of any mental act), all three types of phenomena share the same uniform consciousness. The individual species of consciousness (inner perception) are analogous to one another. For example, judgment (acceptance of rejection) has the same property of consciousness as love and hate.

We will deal with the phenomenon of judgment in the theory of knowledge (Chapter 3), and the phenomenon of love and hate in ethics (Chapter 5).

Endnotes

[1] Franz Brentano, *Psychology from an Empirical Standpoint*, translated by Antos C. Rancurello, D.B. Terrell and Linda López McAlister (from the edition of Oskar Kraus dated in 1924), Routledge & Kegan Paul, New York 1973.

[2] Brentano, *Lectures on Metaphysics*, manuscript B16497 of *Brentano Archiv, in Forsschungstelle für Österreiche philosophie Dokumentationszentrum*, Graz.
[3] Brentano, *Psychology*, p. 23.
[4] Brentano, *Psychology*, p. 5.
[5] Brentano, *Psychology*, p.8.
[6] Brentano, *Psychology*, p. 19.
[7] Brentano, *Psychology*, p.9
[8] Brentano, *Psychology*, p. 20.
[9] Brentano, *Psychology*, p. 10.
[10] Franz Brentano, *Aristotle and His World View*, edited and translated by Rolf George and Roderick M. Chisholm, University of California Press, Berkeley, 1978, p.25.
[11] Brentano, *Psychology*, p. 12.
[12] Cf. Franz Brentano, *Descriptive Psychology*, translated and edited by Benito Müller, New York, Routledge, 1995.
[13] Roderick M. Chisholm, "Brentano's Descriptive Psychology," in L.L. McAlister, p. 91.
[14] Franz Brentano, *Meine letzten Wünsche für Österreich* (Stuttgart, 1895), p. 39.
[15] Cf. Brentano, *Descriptive Psychology*, p. 31-32.
[16] Cf. Brentano, *Psychology*, p. 37-38.
[17] Cf. Franz Brentano, *Origin of our Knowledge of Right and Wrong*, p. 24.
[18] Cf. Brentano, *Descriptive Psychology*, pp. 73-75
[19] Cf. Franz Brentano, *Versuch über die Erkenntnis*, ed. Alfred Kastil (Leibniz, 1925), p. 79.
[20] Cf. Franz Brentano, *Sensory and Noetic Consciousness*, translated by Linda López McAlister, New York, Routledge, 1981, pp. 65-77.
[21] Cf. Franz Brentano, *Aristotle and His World View*, trans. by Rolf George and Roderick Chisholm, University of California Press, Berkeley, 1978, "The Origin of Ideas", p. 36-42. Brentano, *Descriptive Psychology*, p. 173.
[22] Cf. Theodorus de Boer, "Descriptive Method of Franz Brentano: Its Two Functions and Their Significance for Phenomenology," in McAlister, p. 102.
[23] Cf. Brentano, *Psychology*, p. 85-88.
[24] Cf. Brentano, *Psychology*, p. 79.
[25] Here, the German word "*Vorstellung*" is translated into English as "presentation" and not "representation" following the practice of the

translation of *Psychology from an Empirical Point of View*.
[26] Brentano, *Psychology*, p. 88.
[27] Brentano, *Psychology*, p. 88.
[28] Cf. Brentano, *Psychology*, p. 89-91.
[29] The current interpretation of intentionality as a feature of language seems to have its origin in Chisholm, who turned Brentano's notion of intentionality into a feature of language by stating that the sentences we use to talk about mental events have certain logical peculiarities. Chisholm is most interested in the satisfactory logical criteria of intentionality. See Roderick Chisholm, chapter 11 "Intentional Inexistence" of *Perceiving: A Philosophical Study* (Ithaca, N.Y. 1957), pp. 168-185.
[30] Brentano, *Psychology*, p. 91.
[31] Cf. Brentano, *Psychology*, p. 29-30.
[32] Cf. Franz Brentano, *Sensory and Noetic Consciousness*, Edited by Oscar Kraus, Translated by Linda L. McAlister, Routledge & Kegan Paul, New York, 1981, p. 28-38.
[33] Cf. Brentano, *Psychology*, p. 112-113, 118-119, and specially, 405-408.
[34] Cf. Brentano, *Psychology*, Book II, Chapter, IV, pp. 155-176.
[35] Cf. Brentano, *Psychology*, p. 159.
[36] Cf. B. Mijuskowic, "Brentano's Theory of Consciousness," in *Philosophy and Phenomenological Research* 38 (1978): 315-324.
[37] Cf. Franz Brentano, *The Psychology of Aristotle: in Particular his Doctrine of the Active Intellect*, ed. and translated by Rolf George, Berkeley, University of California Press, 1977.
[38] Cf. Carl Stumpf, "Reminiscences of Brentano," in McAlister, (ed.), *The Philosophy of Brentano*, p. 38.
[39] Nevertheless, Brentano rejects the basic Aristotelian classification of faculties in organic faculties and inorganic faculties, that is to say, mental acts which are functions of an organ (seeing, hearing, imagining, etc.), and mental acts which are not functions of an organ (understanding). Cf. Brentano, *Psychology*, p. 195.
[40] Brentano, *Psychology*, p. 194; See pp. 195-197.
[41] Cf. Brentano, *Psychology*, pp.197-200.
[42] Brentano, *Psychology*, p. 198.
[43] Against E. Anscombe's opinion, Brentano explicitly distinguishes between will and feeling. Cf. Brentano, *Psychology*, p. 199.
[44] Brentano, *Psychology*, p. 199.

3
Theory of Knowledge

Brentano's theory of knowledge is connected and well integrated with his psychology. Brentano, in his theory of knowledge, approaches many subjects that have connections not only with his psychology but also with his ethics, aesthetics, and metaphysics. Here we will constrain ourselves to a few central topics. We will start with Brentano's aporia about knowledge, which is formulated in the following way:

(1) APORIA: My ability to know is not something I can trust absolutely, but neither is it something I can prove apodictically. If I want to prove it, I would have to make use of the same ability to know, whose reliability I want to prove. Because of this vicious circle, I can never be reliably certain of any knowledge.[1]

Brentano resolves this aporia in a way that will be the *Leiv Motiv* of his entire theory of knowledge.

(2) MAIN ARGUMENT: If a proposition is directly evident, it will not be necessary to prove the certainty of our knowledge. Therefore, one can trust the ability to know.

(3) NON CIRCULARITY: In (2) there is no circular reasoning like in (1): Although it is true to a certain degree that we fall back on the reliability of our powers of knowledge insofar as we use them. There is only circularity if one premise of an argument is in some way included in the conclusion. Nevertheless, the ability to know is not used as a premise of any argument, so there is no circular reasoning. To use something is not a premise for any argument. Here, Brentano is distinguishing between an activity that is used and an activity that is signified. Only what is signified can be a logical part of a premise. Now, using an activity (such as knowledge) is not to signify it, so it cannot be a premise for any reasoning.

In order to explain the meaning of (2), we have to see what

is directly evident for Brentano, but before dealing with this subject, we have to go to Brentano's theory of judgment, which plays a central role in the question of evidence.

1. The Theory of Judgment

Brentano holds a very idiosyncratic theory of judgment, which has deep ramifications in his whole philosophy. The first thing one has to know about Brentano's theory of judgment —as an important departure from Aristotle's theory of judgment— can be summarized in two statements:

(a) *Judgment is an irreducible psychical act whose object is reality.*
(b) *Perception is synonymous with judgment.*

Statement (a) was established in his psychology, and I will not deal with it here. Statement (b) is essential for Brentano's philosophy. There is an important difference between mere presenting (seeing) a color and perceiving that one is presenting (seeing) a color. The difference is fundamental for Brentano. In perceiving that one is presenting a color, the object is present as something real and indubitable; that is to say, we have here a knowledge of reality, which is a unique characteristic of a judgment (simple presentations and emotions do not intend reality as their specific object.) Therefore, inner perception is a case of a judgment. From here, we draw the conclusion that *the self-consciousness of each psychical act is a judgment.* In this sense, external presentation is not strictly a perception because there is no knowledge of something as existing. The external perception of a color, for instance, is not a perception of the existential reality of color, because colors are only phenomena. For Brentano, only inner perception is strictly perception, while external perception is simply and purely external presentation of a phenomenon without affirming its reality.

The most elementary affirmative existential judgment is manifested as sense consciousness. We are not conscious of our sensations if they are not accompanied by an existential judgment. It is impossible, so Brentano claims, to experience that we are having a sensation without affirming the existence of that sensation.

The differentiating characteristic of an act of judgment from any other psychical act is that it is an act of assent. This

Theory of Knowledge

assent can be of acceptance or rejection of an object previously presented.[2] Now, to accept or to reject an object is synonymous to accepting it as real or to rejecting it as real. A judgment is just the act of assent, *a personal acceptance or rejection* of the object previously presented. For example, the judgment "there are black swans" is an acceptance of black swans as real.

This theory is extremely different from the classic notion of judgment that is conceived as something logical. Classic logic does not study the judgment as a psychological act but as a proposition. Aristotle, for example, describes judgment as the composition or separation of a subject and a predicate. Brentano, on the contrary, rejects the idea of proposition as an object of judgment with the structure of subject and predicate. Brentano holds that the content (or object) of a judgment is not a proposition but something real. The main reason why Brentano rejects the venerable idea of a proposition as such is that he does not accept *irrealia,* inexistent objects. And a proposition as such is not an existent object, but if a proposition is an object of judgment, it has to be an inexistent object, an *irreale,* something that Brentano does not accept. For Brentano, like for some analytic philosophers (such as Russell), only real objects can be objects of our understanding. Brentano will try to prove that a proposition as the object or content of a judgment is purely and simply a *linguistic illusion,* something that abbreviates our mode of communication.

We will start with four proofs for the non-propositional character of the object of judgment:

(1) *Proof by analysis of the existential proposition.*[3] Assume the existential proposition "A exists." Here there is no predicate attributed to a subject; that is, existence is not a predicate said of the subject A. There is no affirmation of a relation between A and existence either, but simply the affirmation (acceptance) of A. The same occurs when we affirm that "A does not exist," what is rejected is not the attribution of existence to A, but simply the rejection of A. A proposition is just a linguistic device to express a psychological phenomenon and to make communication easier.

Brentano's argument runs as follows: Whenever someone affirms a combination of attributes, he simultaneously affirms each particular element of the combination. For example, in

Theory of Knowledge

affirming the existence of a wise man, one affirms both elements, man and wise. If we apply this to "A exists," then we are affirming the existence and A, but in doing so, we are just including the affirmation of A. And what is the difference between affirming A and affirming that "A exists"? Brentano does not see any difference. In other words, A alone is the object of the judgment, which accepts it or rejects it.

This proof is clearer with the negative existential proposition. Assume "A does not exist." First, Brentano establishes the general principle: Whenever someone rejects a combination of attributes he does not reject each particular element of the combination but only the combination. For example, in the proposition "A wise bird does not exist" we do not reject bird as such and wise as such, which both exist, but the combination. Then, Brentano applies this principle to the example "A does not exist." And in applying that principle Brentano finds the following result: If the proposition "A does not exist" were the denial of a combination of the predicate existence to the subject A, then A would not be denied in any way, which is precisely what we expected. This is absurd; therefore, the object of judgment—"A does not exist"— does not have a propositional structure.

In conclusion, (a) any judgment is only the affirmation or rejection of the existence of the subject. If one says "Peter is a professor," he is affirming the professor Peter; he is saying that the professor Peter exists. (b) The existential judgment is not a categorical judgment, the copula "is" lacks significance as such. It does not put the subject and the predicate (existence) together; there is no synthesis of A and existence but just acceptance or rejection of A.

(2) *Proof by the identification of perception with judgment.* That predication is not the essence of a judgment can be internally perceived in the phenomenon of inner perception, which is, for Brentano, a type of judgment. Inner perception, Brentano holds, is not the conjunction of a concept —the subject— and another concept —the predicate. The object of an inner perception is simply a phenomenon—a psychical phenomenon. But the analysis of this phenomenon does not yield anything such as a predication. *Perception is just the acceptance of what was previously presented without adding anything to the*

Theory of Knowledge

content presented. When we perceive internally that I am seeing a colored surface, the object of my inner perception is the act of seeing, and to perceive internally my act of seeing is the same as to accept the reality or existence of my act of seeing. In other words, when I am seeing a colored surface, I notice that I am seeing, I notice the existence and reality of my act of seeing. Maybe the colored surface does not correspond to any extramental reality as Brentano holds, but I know that my act of seeing is a reality with effective existence because it is an act that I notice I am performing. Now, if inner perception is just the acceptance of the reality or existence of a mental act when something extramental is presented, then the concept of existence comes directly from experience, that is to say, from the experience of inner perception. In this whole description, Brentano did not use any predication, and he explained perception without adding any predicative structure, and what the description of inner perception yields is enough to explain its nature without any recourse to a predicative structure.

(3) *Proof by the analysis of existence.* In the traditional account of a judgment, existence is seen as a predicate. For example, "the planet Jupiter exists," in the traditional logic, "exists" functions as a predicate. On the contrary, Brentano wants to show that the analysis of the concept of existence yields the conclusion that the object of a judgment is not a predication. In one of the rare concessions to Kant's critical philosophy,[4] Brentano accepts that existence is not a real predicate, although Brentano's argumentation is very different from Kant's. Let us see how Brentano arrives at this idea.

First of all, there is no concept of existence prior to judgment, thus, there is no way of attributing the concept of existence to a subject. *The phenomenon of existence is not a physical phenomenon.* We see colors, hear sounds, etc., but the phenomenon of existence is not among them. It is obvious that we have the concept of existence, but it is not obtained from any physical phenomenon. We obtain the concept of existence after performing a judgment, or clearer, an affirmation or acceptance of a content, that is to say, the acceptance of an object previously presented. How do we obtain the concept of existence from an acceptance? By means of a reflection. The concept of existence rises when one reflects on the act of acceptance, which is the

Theory of Knowledge

essence of a judgment.

Brentano's position about existence can be formulated in the following way: (a) Existence is not the content of any judgment because the experience of judgment does not have propositions as objects, the only place in which existence could be a content of a judgment. (b) The idea of existence does not come from the content of the object judged, but from the *form* of the judgment —the act of acceptance. Thus, *existence is the form of a judgment*; that is to say, existence is the way by which the object is conceived in the act of judging. In phenomenological parlance, these kinds of judgments are called "thetics." The existential judgment "A exists" is thetic because it affirms or "puts" the existence of A. Brentano did not use this terminology but it seems to be very akin to his intention. Brentano understands existence as a form that all judgments acquire when they accept the object. To affirm an object is tantamount to putting the object as real.

What Brentano very probably has in mind about existence has connections with Kant and Aristotle. For Kant, categories are forms of judgment, among them existence is a category, a form. The matter of a judgment is the content received from sense intuition. The category of existence is an *a priori* form that is imposed on the sense content. Now, Brentano seems to have this in mind, but he rejects any kind of Kantian *a priori* forms. Existence has to come from empirical sources; existence is not an *a priori* form of our intellect. In this sense, Brentano is under Aristotelian influence, but with the important difference that Brentano does not admit an external perception of existence, so existence has to come from inner perception. As a result, existence is the form that a judgment obtains when it accepts an object.

The most interesting conclusion from these ideas can be summarized in three points: (a) *existence comes from experience*, not from external but from internal experience, and (b) not from the content of the inner experience or perception but (c) from the reflection on this experience. To exist is said of everything that can be affirmed or accepted correctly.

Given this account of existence, the next logical step for Brentano is the equation between truth and existence. Brentano holds that to say that "A exists" is the same as to affirm or ac-

Theory of Knowledge

cept A, and this is identical to saying that A is true. For example, the judgment "some man is sick" is a linguistic abbreviation of "a sick man exists," which is equivalent to "there is a sick man," or "the fact that there is a sick man," or "it is true that there is a sick man," all these forms are interchangeable. So, for Brentano, existence is another way of expressing the truth of a judgment. We will say more about this when we arrive to Brentano's metaphysics.

(4) *Proof that judgments are not predicamental by the fact that it is possible to reduce all predication to existential propositions.*[5] We saw that all existential propositions are not genuine propositions but existential judgments in which we accept the content of something presented previously. Now, Brentano's strategy is to reduce all kinds of predication to existential predication, and thus, to reduce every judgment to its essence —acceptance— which is non-predicative. If Brentano is successful in doing this, then all judgments have a non-predicative structure.

Brentano will show that all categorical propositions are existential propositions by reducing each one of the four classic judgments to existential judgments. The following figure is the traditional square of propositions from which Brentano will start the transformation of all propositions to non-propositional existential judgments:

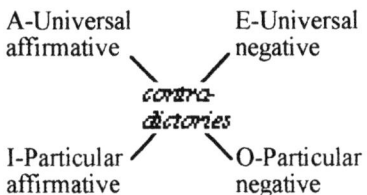

- Universal affirmative proposition (A): "Every man is mortal" = "There is no immortal man"
- Universal negative proposition (E): "No stone is alive" = "there is no living stone"
- Particular affirmative proposition (I): "Some men are sick" = "there is a sick man"
- Particular negative proposition (O): "Some men are wise" = "There is a non-wise man".

Theory of Knowledge

The expressions "there is" and "there is no" of these existential propositions are placed instead of the copula of a proposition. This means that the meaning of the copula in any proposition is completely void; it does not have any real significance. It is only a linguistic abbreviation.

One can think that it is easy to criticize this theory by showing that Brentano cannot completely get rid of the synthesis between the predicate and subject. In some way, there is a composition or synthesis of subject and predicate that Brentano tries to avoid. Let us see the objection. The transformation from "A person is wise" into "A wise person exists" assumes the synthesis between "person" and "wise," which is the essence of predication. Brentano replies that this is certainly a synthesis, but it is not realized in the judgment but earlier in the most elemental mental act —the presentation. The judgment limits itself to affirming the complex content ("a wise person") presented previously. The novelty of this theory is that the synthesis is given by the presentation, while in Kant and Aristotle, the synthesis is produced in the level of judgment. Brentano here seems to reduce all prepositional synthesis to complex concepts. Some prominent medieval philosophers (such as Aquinas) held that the result of a judgment is always a complex concept, for example, the result of the judgment "a person is wise" is the complex concept "a wise person", but the synthesis was made in the judgment, while Brentano holds that the synthesis is already produced in the presentation; the judgment does not produce any synthesis but affirms the synthesis.

2. Theory of Terms

In designing his theory of judgment, Brentano took care to avoid any kind of *irrealia*, that is to say, any kind of unreal objects. This was the main motive for not accepting the predicational theory of judgment in which the subject of a true predication could be entities which are unreal objects, and the predication as an object of judgment is another unreal object. For example, the proposition "five is a prime number" is true. What this implies is that the subject "five" is an unreal object; it is an object that does not exist. But Brentano thinks that it is very problematic to believe in a Platonic cosmos in which these

Theory of Knowledge

unreal and ideal objects are placed. Thus, he prefers to transform the predicational theory of judgment into one which is not predicational but thetic. So, Brentano transforms the above example into "there is not a no-prime number five," in which one rejects that object without being committed to the being of unreal objects such as numbers. The same thing occurs in relation to the proposition as an object of judgment. For example, the proposition "a horse is running" taken as an object of judgment is an unreal object, an object that does not exist; what exists is the running horse but the whole object a-horse-is-running neither runs nor is alive but is an *irreale*. If we transform these propositions into non-propositional content *à la* Brentano, we seem to get rid of any unreal object.

The theory of judgment implies, in turn, a theory about the terms which are involved in the judgment. Brentano distinguishes between genuine terms and non-genuine terms. Genuine terms are those which refers to real entities. (Let me reiterate again that, for Brentano, what is real is only that which is individual and concrete versus what is unreal such as universals and abstracts.) All genuine terms refer to individuals. What happens then with fictional terms like "Pegasus," "Hamlet," etc.? Brentano does not hesitate to indicate that they refer to real individuals as well. And here is where the genius of our philosopher is manifested. These terms are genuine terms if there is a person who accepts or rejects them. An acceptor is a person who makes a positive judgment about the object of a term, and a rejector is a person who makes a negative judgment about the object of a term. Now we have all the elements to explain why fictional terms refer to real things:

(a) A person who thinks that there are horses is a "horse-acceptor" and a person who thinks that Pegasus does not exist is a "Pegasus-rejector."

(b) In cases of fictional terms such as "Pegasus" what the term refers to is not a inexistent object called "Pegasus" but to the person who rejects the object Pegasus, the Pegasus-rejector, which is always real, a concrete and individual thing.

3. Truth and Evidence

For Brentano, the essence of judgment is

Theory of Knowledge

acceptance/rejection, but another essential characteristic of all judgments is their relation to truth. Since Aristotle, it has become common doctrine that the judgment is the proper place for truth, and when we are talking about truth in other senses (for example, a true sensation, a true dollar bill, a true person, and so on) it is a derivative truth, a truth that, in the end, is borrowed from a judgment, that is to say, the truth of these things comes from a true judgment.

Brentano distinguishes two kinds of judgments: blind judgment and evident judgment. A blind judgment is a judgment that is true but there is no strict evidence of its truth. We assume it is true, and probably it is, but we can not prove it apodictically. (a) Brentano thinks that most of the judgments based on external perception (judgments about the physical world) are blind judgments. For example, the judgment that the external world contains tridimensional bodies is highly probable (at least more probable than its alternative), but it is not strictly evident; we cannot prove it apodictically but only with a degree of probability. But, so Brentano says, this is enough to trust in these blind judgments. (b) Judgments based on memory are blind as well. Memory is not a reliable source of evidence, memory too often fails. But many of the judgments based on memory are probably true inasmuch as they confirm each other. Although this knowledge is not evident, it deserves our confidence and trust, with a grain of salt.

An evident judgment can be of two types: directly evident and indirectly evident. A judgment is indirectly evident if the evidence is borrowed from another judgment. Usually, we have an indirectly evident judgment in conclusions of a syllogism, inference from axioms, and in general, in the conclusion of a valid argument where the conclusion is not evident by itself but from the premises. For example, the Pythagorean theorem $a^2+b^2=c^2$ is indirectly evident, its evidence comes from other evident judgments, which are the premises of the argument that arrives at the Pythagorean conclusion.

An indirectly evident judgment cannot depend on another judgment which, in turn, is indirectly evident depending on another judgment which is indirectly evident, to infinity. If this were the case, the whole series of judgments would be indirectly evident, that is to say, the whole series would depend on nothing, which is absurd. In the end, we have to arrive at some evidence which is not borrowed from another judgment From here, Brentano claims we have to admit another class of judgments which are directly evident.

Directly evident judgments can be of two types. The first type are *judgments of inner perception*, which constitute the inner consciousness of each psychical phenomena. These kinds of judgments are indubitable, and their evidence is directly grasped. For example, "I am seeing that this piece of paper is on the table" is a judgment of inner perception which is directly evident. The evidence is not about the existence of the piece of paper nor the existence of the table nor any physical object but the existence of the psychical act of seeing. My mental act of seeing is evident for me while I am seeing the object piece of paper on the table. To illustrate this consider these two statements:

(1) The piece of paper is on the table
(2) I am seeing the piece of paper on the table

Statement (1) is not directly evident (nor indirectly but perhaps probable) because maybe I am deceived by my senses; on the contrary, statement (2) is always directly evident because I am not judging the existence of the piece of paper on the table but my act of seeing that I am perceiving internally while I am having the experience of seeing, in other words, I "feel" my act of seeing when I am now seeing a physical object. If I were not conscious of my act of seeing, I could not say that I am now seeing the piece of paper on the table.

The second type of directly evident judgments are *judgments of reasons* or *insights*, which are analytic judgments. For example, red is different from green, the whole is greater than the parts, two things are more than one thing, a triangle has three sides, and so on. All these judgments are directly evident by analysis of the concept of red and green, whole and part, two and one, triangle, and so on. Axioms of logic belong to this kind of judgments (Brentano has in mind the Aristotelian logic in which axioms are evident).

From this analysis we have that a judgment can be true, but it does not mean that it is evident because all judgments that are evident have to be true. A blind judgment, for example, is true but it is not evident for us. What it is not

Theory of Knowledge

possible in Brentano's account is an evident judgment which is false. This point is important because this is what differentiates Brentano's theory of judgment from relativism. Brentano holds that if a person judges with evidence —say, direct evidence— the judgment is true, and every person would be able to have this evident judgment, or better, what is directly evident for one is directly evident for any person. Let us look at this point more specifically .

Truth belongs to the judgment of a person who judges correctly, which is the judgment of one who asserts what the person who judges with evidence would assert. For example, to say that A exists is tantamount to saying that anyone who judged about A with evidence would accept A, and to say that A does not exist is tantamount to saying that anyone who judged about A with evidence would reject A. This doctrine, so Brentano claims, is the correct variation of Protagoras's saying, now modified by Brentano: "*the man who judges with evidence is the measure of all things.*"

Now, we have a problem with this last conclusion. Why is this conclusion not a form of relativism like Protagoras' doctrine? Brentano firmly rejects any kind of relativism as a weak and unstable epistemological theory. To say that the person who judges with evidence is the measure of truth is not relativism because it is not possible that a person affirming a situation with evidence can reject the same situation with evidence: this is a contradiction. Now, why is it not possible to have contradictory, evident judgments about the same situation? Remember Locke's experiment, in which we feel a higher temperature in the hand that is cold and we feel a lower temperature in the other hand that is warm. If the person who judges with evidence is the measure of what is truth, is not Locke's experiment a refutation of Brentano's theory of directly evident judgments?

The answer to this question is already implicit in Brentano's theory of judgment. From his theory of non-propositional judgment, Brentano can give a satisfactory account of what he previously called "directly evident." Because his theory of judgment is based on *personal* acceptance or rejection, it is easy to see that the act of accepting a certain object is the contrary of the act of rejecting that object, and it is

Theory of Knowledge

impossible for a person to make contradictory judgments at one and the same time. It is impossible to both accept a certain object and *at one and the same time* to reject that object. This is because the *same person* cannot have two contradictory acts simultaneously, one of acceptance and the other of rejection. Contradictory things cannot exist, and this is apodictically true. Therefore, a person cannot judge contradictory situations with evidence. Obviously, this line of argument is not possible with a theory of judgment based on propositions; and this is a point that Brentano exploits very often.

As one can easily notice, Brentano is giving priority to the principle of contradiction over any other thing. This is not a problem for what is directly evident because the logical axioms (judgments of reason or insights) are directly evident as well, and probably Brentano thought about them as regulative of inner perception, which are directly evident judgments.

The evidence occurring with axioms and other judgments of reason stems not from a blind psychological compulsion, or a feeling (like in Hume), or an impulse to believe, or a degree of subjective conviction, or any other subjectivist explanation, but from their own inner self-illuminating evidence. To say, Brentano argues, that I could be so constructed that I must agree with what is false, is the same thing as saying, I am uncertain whether that which I am certain of might not be false, something that is a completely absurd.

Brentano sides with all philosophers who boldly say that neither nature nor God deceived us. Even God cannot make it evident to us that green is the sound of a flute or 2+1=4. This means that God's will would thereby contradict itself. Brentano claims that it is inappropriate to say that this impossibility in God diminishes God's power because this impossibility does not deny God's perfection but rather His imperfection. Brentano here alludes to a well-known medieval controversy on which Descartes took an affirmative position (God can create contradictions) and Leibniz a negative position (God cannot create contradictions such as a circular square, or to make evil good). Brentano, therefore, is in agreement with Leibniz. In addition, Brentano says that the directly evident judgment is true not only for our human intellects but *for any possible intellect* because it is only the illumination of the

Theory of Knowledge

content itself. Something is evident because of the content and not because of one's peculiar psychological complexion. This proves that Brentano was worlds away from a relativist psychologism, which tries to derive evidence from psychological compulsion.[6]

In the development of his theory of judgment, Brentano later became interested in the new doctrine of modality. He distinguished sharply between the concepts of evident, sureness, certainty, and exactness, which many philosophers had more or less put in the same group of the apodictic judgment.

• *Sureness* = degrees of probability, as one of the characteristics rooted in the content or object of the judgment. Brentano became interested in developing a theory of knowledge based on mathematical probabilities.

• *Certainty or conviction* = subjective characteristic of a judgment that is also dependent upon feelings, important in religious belief. This is not to be confused with evidence, which is not a feeling *a la* Hume as we saw before.

4. Analytic and *A Priori* Judgments

Contrary to Kant, analytic judgments extend our knowledge. One of the favorite examples of Brentano is with colors. For example, "Whatever is violet is red and blue" is a case of analytic judgment that Brentano frequently uses. Given that physically violet is a compound color made up of red and blue, (all compound color are made up of a combination of primary colors); so, Brentano claims, red and blue are *analytic* elements of violet, that is to say. Now, one who knows that a certain thing is violet without knowing that is made out of red and blue may be enlightened when told, analytically, that violet is red and blue, that is to say, the judgment "whatever is violet is red and blue" is analytic and increases our knowledge. Another example, the statement "all cubes have twelve edges", that for Kantian philosophers is described as being synthetic *a priori*, would also express an analytic judgment, according to Brentano. The analysis of the concept cube yields that it has twelve edges just as the analysis of the concept violet yields that it is made up of red and blue. Such judgments extend our knowledge since they enable us to transform a confused

Theory of Knowledge

perception into one that is clear and distinct.[7] One who does not know mathematics may have a confused perception of cube; so, if the person is enlightened, he will see that the concept of cube yields that it has twelve edges.

A priori judgments are self-evident simply in virtue of the analysis of the concepts involved in the judgment, but —and what follows is important in Brentano's philosophy— *to disclose the a priori is not an aprioristic construction* (like in Kant and Husserl). Analytic judgments increase our knowledge of reality (this is established in open opposition to Kant's doctrine). This is possible because the content of these concepts comes itself from reality. Although the judgment that analyzes the concepts is *a priori*, the concept itself is empirical. For example, "red is different from green" is *a priori* and analytic, but the concepts of red and green have an empirical origin, but once we get them, it is *a priori* and analytic that red is different from green, that is to say, the comparison that our mind makes of them is based on the analysis of these concepts.

Brentano, as an empiricist *suo generis*, bases all knowledge on experience. The genius of Brentano is to recognize only perception as the source of all knowledge (for Brentano, all knowledge begins and arises from experience like in Aristotle and Hume), while other philosophers, such as Husserl, feel obliged to admit other sources of knowledge different from perception, such as the intuition of essences, to justify *a priori* knowledge.

Endnotes

[1] Cf. Carl Stumpf, "Reminiscences of Franz Brentano", in *The Philosophy of Franz Brentano*, p. 17.
[2] In German, Brentano uses "*Anerkennung*" and "*Verwerfung,*" which we translated into "acceptance" and "rejection" respectively.
[3] Cf. Brentano, *Psychology*, Book II, Chapter VIII, § 5, p. 208ff
[4] Cf. Brentano, *Psychology*, p. 211.
[5] Cf. Brentano, *Psychology*, p. 210-221.
[6] Cf. Stumpf, "Reminiscences of Franz Brentano", in The Philosophy of Franz Brentano, p. 17-18.
[7] Cf. Franz Brentano, *Versuch über die Erkenntnis*, ed. Alfred Kastil, Leipzig, 1925, pp. 9ff.

4
Metaphysics

It is a common idea about Brentano's philosophy that psychology was the starting point of his systematic philosophizing. Although psychology effectively played a very important role in his philosophy, metaphysics was the beginning and the end of his thought. The deepest and innermost driver of Brentano's philosophy was essentially metaphysics; even his descriptive psychology, which methodologically removes metaphysical elements, is only a necessary step oriented to a metaphysical goal. Brentano declared to one of his students that "I am at the moment wholly a metaphysician ... I must confess that, after having been exclusively a psychologist for a few years, the change makes me happy."[1]

The starting point of Brentano's metaphysics is Aristotle, but includes important elements from medieval metaphysics and Leibniz's metaphysics as well. Brentano deviated from his Aristotelian roots gradually over his lifetime, but only if he saw compelling reasons for doing so. As in his psychology, the method of metaphysics is the same as that of the natural sciences, *viz.* the empirical method.[2]

All of Brentano's metaphysical work starts from his dissertation *On the Several Senses of Being in Aristotle* (1862), and even, I would say, his whole philosophy barrows many insights from this work. In discussing Brentano's metaphysics, it seems logical to start from his interpretation of Aristotle's notion of being, then we will jump to his last conception of metaphysics, which is found in *The Doctrine of Categories*. We will finish his metaphysics with some remarks about the existence of God.

1. The Fourfold Distinction of Being

In his study of Aristotle's metaphysics, Brentano found that something is said to "be" in at least four ways or senses: (1) Accidental being, for example, "Socrates is wise," the quality wise is predicated accidentally (or incidentally) of the subject Socrates; that is to say, "wise" is not an essential property of the humanity of Socrates; (2) being in the sense of being true, and non-being in the sense of being false, for example, "Socrates is wise," in which the propositional copula "is" expresses the fact of being true that Socrates is wise; (3) being

60

Metaphysics

as potency and act, for example, "Socrates is thinking," "thinking" is an act of Socrates, or Socrates is in actuality thinking; (4) being as the different categories (substance and accidents).[3] These four general ways or senses in which being is said of or attributed to something can be reduced to two types: physical (or real) being and logical (or unreal) being. In Brentano's interpretation, these two types are irreducible to each other, although logical being is based on the physical or real being, because for Aristotle logic mirrors reality and unlike in the work of modern philosophers, such as Kant, logic no longer mirrors reality, and there is even a strong possibility that reality mirrors logic. In other words, for Aristotle, the logical being depends on the physical or real being because our thoughts depend on reality. For our purposes, I will restrict myself to being as the categories and being as true and false as mentioned above.

Being as being true and non-being as being false take place properly and mainly in judgment. This means that truth and falsity are not in things but in our mind which judges a thing. If sometimes things are called true or false (for example, true gold), they are called so with respect to our judgment of that thing. For example, gold is physically what it is, gold, and only for us, something is real gold if the appearance is what it represents. This type of being is important because it resolves paradoxes such as "nothing *is* nothing," in which it is said that "nothing" *is* ... But this "is" is only propositional, it expresses the truth of that proposition. Because of this, Aristotle calls this being in the sense of being true.[4]

Being according to the figures of the categories are irreducible kinds of real beings. As Brentano puts it, the categories are the highest univocal general concepts or the highest genera of being real. Brentano gathers a list of Aristotelian categories such as substance, relations, qualities, quantity, action, and affection, etc. The interesting point Brentano is making in his study is that Aristotle arrived to the list of categories according to the different manners of predication.[5] And because there are two types of predications, *viz.* essential and accidental predication, there will be two types of categories: substance and accidents. So, a category falls under the concept of substance or under the concept of accident.

In the history of philosophy, there were many different views about the nature of a substance. Locke conceived of a substance as what hides behind the sense phenomena and links these sense phenomena together. Leibniz, closer to Aristotle than Locke, conceives of a substance as a monad, which is a unitary and simple thing (without parts), incorruptible, ingenerable, with mental properties (perception). Kant, on the contrary, conceived of substance as that which remains

Metaphysics

identical through change and time, but with an important difference in relation to the Aristotelian view: substance is nothing real but a category of the intellect, a form which we apply to the data coming from our senses. Brentano rejects all these conceptions of substance and prefers to start from Aristotle's notion of substance.

According to Brentano, the Aristotelian categories are:

(1) Accidents: quality, quantity, where, when, action and reaction, affection, position and state or habit. For example, running is an action and an accident of an animal, smiling is another action and an accident of a human person. Others accidents are not actions but something static such as the redness (quality) of a child's cheek, the height (quantity) of a tree, and so on.

(2) Substance: it is the bearer of accidents and what serves to individuate one accident from another (for example, the color green is individually different in different individuals but qualitatively the same. This means that the substance of a plant is not only the bearer of the quality green and other accidents such as height but it individuates this green from other greens in other substances.

Now, if the differences of the proper manners of predication, in general, correspond to the differences between the categories, then we have here that predication is what provides a logical unity to all categories. This is the reason Brentano puts the following words in Aristotle's mouth: "Aristotle could rightly say that 'being' has as many meanings as there are manners of assertion, i.e., manners in which one thing can be predicated of another, and that the highest genera must be distinguished in the same way in which being is divided".[6] Certainly, Brentano rejects the idea that the categories are only manners of predication. They are more than that; they are manners of being real. But there is in Brentano's exposition a certain tendency to place the unity of all categories in the mind that predicates, or better, in the mind that judges with truth that something is predicated of something. For example, Brentano maintains that the difference between categories is not necessarily a real difference, but a rational or logical difference,[7] something that corroborates the idea that predication is more important than reality in order to classify the categories, and in general, to classify the several senses of being. On the contrary, in the conclusion of his study on Aristotle, Brentano faces the question of the regulating viewpoint of classifying the categories. He rejects the idea that the categories are classified according to grammatical relations and puts the regulating point on the real modes of being. In any case, it seems that Brentano is not sufficiently clear of this issue, and it is not difficult to show some tendency in Brentano's interpretation that the different senses or manners of being are mainly different manners of predication.

Metaphysics

If my claim is right, Brentano seems to be interpreting Aristotle as saying that the several senses or manners of being fall under a single concept of being because they fall under a true predication. Therefore, being as being true and non-being as being false is the logical connection of all senses or manners of being. This conclusion can explain why Brentano's view of existence is closely related to the notion of truth.

2. Reism

The term "reism" was coined by Tadeusz Kotarbinski and it was applied to Brentano's metaphysics. Reism is the doctrine by which there are no objects other than things. Brentano, in this sense, is a reist. He does not admit universals, abstracts as objects, and everything that is an object of thought is always a thing. As we saw earlier, a thing for Brentano is every individual object, and this is the realm of reality. No things are unreal; they not only do not have being, but they are not objects of thought either.

What is the difference between reism and materialism? For a materialist only material objects are things, and they exhaust the realm of reality. On the contrary, for a reist, material objects are not the only objects that exhaust the concept of reality. Reality embraces both material things and immaterial things. The examples of immaterial things are mental acts, the human soul and God. So, although Brentano only admits things as reality, things are not only material.

A better term for Brentano's position would have been the term "concretism" because only concrete objects are things, and abstract and universal objects are purely and simply linguistic fictions. Concretism has the advantage over reism that objects of imagination fall under a concrete object, so they are things for Brentano. But the term "reism" is awkward to apply to objects of imagination. For example, the Centaur is an object that does not exist, but as far as it is an object of imagination it is a concrete object.[8] Nevertheless, I will use both terms "reism" and "concretism" interchangeably.

The reason Brentano admits imaginary objects as real objects is that it is not impossible that they exist. For example, the Unicorn is a fictional object, but it is a concrete object too, it could exist. It is a fact that the Centaur does not exist, but the existence of such a creature is not absolutely impossible, and if it could exist, it is because it is a concrete individual from the beginning. The same thing happens with all objects of imagination. On the contrary, universals and abstracts cannot exist at all. Whiteness is not only inexistent, it cannot exist. The universal man is by definition non-concrete and non-individual, and as a consequence, it is impossible that a universal man can exist.

Metaphysics

What exists is this man called Peter, or that man called John, but not man as such. All existent objects are always concrete objects, individual objects. Thus, the concept of real becomes the fundamental concept of metaphysics and the only true object of thought.

Specifically, Brentano's reism is a doctrine and a program. The doctrine says that *only individual things exist and only things can be objects of thought*; the program is ruled by a critique of language (*Sprachkritik*) or analysis of language, in which Brentano proposes to transform all propositions containing abstract names (*i.e.* names which are not referring to things) into propositions containing only real names (*i.e.* names which refer to things or individual and concrete objects). It is a fact that ordinary language appears to contain names that designate all sorts of unreal objects. The program of a linguistic analysis is to show that our thought can afford to do without these unreal objects, that all such references can be eliminated by a transformation into a language containing only the names of real things, essentially persons and physical things. Brentano's critique of language (in a way that anticipates Russell's analysis) has the role of an Ockham's razor.

Brentano, influenced by his disciple Anton Marty's analysis of language, maintained that language works according to fictions and treats pseudo-objects (i.e. universals, abstracts, etc.) as if they were things. This is due to the nature of a term, which is endowed with a content, which moves the mind to assume that there is always a thing as referent. Based on linguistic analysis of philosophy, Brentano thinks that abstract names have no autonomous meaning, but are connected with other names that have an autonomous meaning. Brentano called these names that do not have an autonomous meaning "synsemantics".

What is the meaning of "synsemantic"? In some way, what Brentano has in mind reminds us of what Wittgenstein says years later, Brentano's analysis of language tries to unveil the true meaning of words and to show the thought that words covert and hide. In the language we use, each word is worlds away from having a meaning by itself, an autonomous meaning. What defines an object signified by a word is the network formed by several words bound to each other. Brentano mentions the example of prepositions and conjunctions in propositional language. Here, prepositions and conjunctions do not have any meaning in isolation, by themselves, autonomously. Prepositions and conjunctions are synsemantic (meaning-with), that is to say, their meaning depends of the meaning of other words.[9]

In addition to this, language very often uses fictions to abbreviate a complicated thought. For example, mathematics talks of negative numbers, imaginary numbers, etc., which are only linguistic uses,

Metaphysics

which, in the strict sense of the words, are improper. When we use abstract words, we are inclined to use them autosemantically (with meaning of their own), that is to say, as if these words express abstract objects, but in reality these words have to be taken as linguistic fictions, with the role of simplifying our complex thoughts. In themselves, abstract words do not have any autonomous meaning, they are synsemantic. Brentano mentions a long list of words that are synsemantic. I will mention some of them that fit our purpose: the past and the future, non existence, possibility, qualities, etc.

In these cases, what exists is only the subject that thinks of them. Brentano claims that in all cases in which I believe that I am thinking of an unreal object I cannot think about it without reference to a subject —myself— that is the thinker.

We can summarize Brentano's reism in two statements: (a) there are only concrete individual things, and (b) every judgment is either the acceptance or the rejection of a concrete individual thing. Here, the term "concrete" has to be taken as the opposite of abstract; therefore, concrete includes not only physical, but also immaterial objects such as mental acts.

Brentano has several arguments to support his reism. Probably the most interesting argument is based on the univocal significance of the term "thinking." Brentano here is using the term "thinking" in a very broad sense (à la Cartesian) meaning any act of presentation. The argument runs as follows:[10]

(1) There is an axiom essential in Brentano's psychology that says "to think is always to think of something." It is not possible to think and to not think of something, just like it is not possible to see without seeing something, or to imagine without imagining something.

(2) Now, the term "to think" is univocal, that is, the use of "to think" is equal to any object. To think (or more technically, to present) of this or that object does not change the nature of thinking. For example, to think of a tree is the same kind of act of thinking as to think of a planet or to think of the color red.

(3) Because to think is always to think of something, if "to think" is univocal, the term "something" has to be univocal as well. Here, Brentano is assuming that there is a 1-1 relation between thinking and the something that is thought.

(4) But there is no generic concept that can be common both to things and to non-things.

(5) Therefore, if "something" denotes a thing at one time, it cannot denote a non-thing at another time, it would be an impossibility if "something" has to remain univocal. Hence, Brentano says that only

Metaphysics

concrete and individual things are objects of our thoughts, and unreal objects are merely fictions of language, although, sometimes, they are very convenient, as seen in mathematics.

To illustrate this argument, we will pretend that Brentano is incorrect in this analysis by showing that there is a more comprehensive class than the class of real things, in such a way that it embraces real things and unreal objects. One logical possibility can be that the term "something" ranges univocally over the class of what is thinkable. Certainly, universals, abstract objects, ideal objects, etc. are as thinkable as real objects. It seems that everything falls under the univocal concept of thinkable. Obviously, Brentano disagrees with this. The reason is as follows:

(1) If being thinkable is acceptable as a characteristic at all, it must indeed be a characteristic that applies generally to everything of which one can be said to be thinking.

(2) Now, *thinkable is not a characteristic of anything*, thinkable is just what medieval philosophers called *"denominatio extrinseca"* (external denomination), which can be discovered by linguistic analysis and shown to be just another linguistic fiction.

What is a *"denominatio extrinseca"* (external denomination)? It means that when we are thinking of, for example, a tree, to be thought of is nothing for the tree, it does not add any weight, any height, and so on. To be thought of is just an external denomination of something that adds nothing to it. That a thing is thinkable means only that somebody has the capacity to think of it, but that capacity is in the person who is thinking and not in the thing that is thought of. Therefore, if thinkable is an external denomination, that is to say, it is not a characteristic of things, then it will not be able to be the univocal concept of object that we were looking for.

This conclusion can be illustrated by two observations. (a) Assume that there is no mind in the universe. So, there will be no thinkable thing either because there is no one with the capacity to think of it. But things would be the same whether there are minds or not. Therefore, thinkable is not a characteristic of things, it cannot be the universal something we were looking for. (b) In addition to this, Brentano observes that when we are thinking of a horse we are not thinking of the thinkability of a horse. If you desire to have a horse, you do not desire the thinkability of the horse, otherwise, you would be satisfied with the possession of the thinkability of the horse, and there would be no necessity to possess the real horse.

3. The Notion of Being

What *is* there in the strict sense of the word? Brentano claims

Metaphysics

that "is" in the strict sense of the word is that which is to be correctly affirmed in the *modus praesens*, that is to say, being is just any thing which is to be correctly affirmed in the *modus praesens*. To understand this claim we have to see what *modus praesens* is.[11]

Brentano has a theory of modes in which an object is thought about or judged. To judge that there *is* A is to accept A in the *modus praesens* (mode of present); to judge that there *was* A is to accept A in the mode of past; and to judge there *will be* A is to accept A in the mode of the future. Now, being in the strict sense of the word can only be correctly accepted or affirmed in the mode of present because past and future objects as past or future do not exist. Past happened, so it *is not* any more, and future will be, so it *is not* yet. Only present is happening, so it *is* in the strict sense of the word.

Brentano distinguishes the term being, in the strict sense, from the term thing. The term "being" applies to any thing that is actual, that is to say, any existing thing. But a thing does not need to be actual; it does not need to be existent. Past things and future things are things but they are not beings in the strict sense. Even an object of imagination, such as the Centaur, is a thing, individual and concrete thing that does not exist. The Centaur is a thing but it is not a being.

Based on the argument of the univocity of the object of thinking given above, Brentano's reism is fully committed to the univocity of existence. Existence or being in the strict sense does not have several meanings like in Aristotle but only one, the effective existence.

If we put together this conception of being with Brentano's theory of judgment, we will have the following results:

(1) "A exists" means that A is such that anyone who judges it with evidence would accept it.

(2) "A does not exist" means that A is such that anyone who judges it with evidence would reject it.

(3) "A did exist" means that A is such that anyone who judges it with evidence would affirm something in the mode of present as being previous to it.

(4) "A will exist" means that A is such that anyone who judges it with evidence would affirm something in the mode of present as being posterior to it.

4. Metaphysics of Accident

One of the senses of being is being as substance and accidents, that is to say, being as the categories, which are modes of being real. Brentano claims that the notion of substance can be better understood only as correlative to that of accidents. If a substance is that which can gain or lose accidents (for example, an animal can gain or lose weight),

Metaphysics

then we are defining what is a substance in relation to its accidents. Therefore, Brentano believes that it is natural to start studying the notion of accident before studying that of a substance.

Among beings in the strict sense of the term, there are to be included substances, aggregates of substances, parts of substances, and accidents (real properties and qualities of things).[12] What kind of thing is an accident? Assume a thing that thinks; the result would be a thinker or a thinking thing. In Brentano's conception of accident, the whole called "thinker" would be an accident of that thing. This accident is something that comes into existence when the thing begins to think, and the accident passes away when the thing ceases to think. If we assume a thing that sees and hears, the result would be two more accidents of this thing, namely, a seeing thing and a hearing thing. Brentano draws interesting conclusions from here:

(1) Both accidents the seeing thing and the hearing thing *are independent* of each other in that either can exist without the other. It is possible to conceive without contradiction that a seeing thing is not a hearing thing and vice versa.

(2) Nevertheless, the seeing thing and the hearing thing *cannot be independent* of the first thing. There are no seeing things without being in a thing and there are no hearing things without being in a thing.

(3) The seeing thing and the hearing thing are accidents of a thing, which is the substance of these accidents. Accidents exist in things, which are called substances or subjects of these accidents.

In the case of a human person, we have that when a person sees, or hears, then the self (the ego, or the "I"), has as accidents a hearer (a seeing thing) and the see-er (a seeing thing), and these accidents can exist independently of each other, but they cannot exist independently of the self, (the ego, or "I"). From here we have that there is a person-who-sees and there is a person-who-hears, and it is possible for each one to fall away and for the other to remain (sometimes we are seeing but not hearing, and vice versa). These two accidents (the seeing thing and the hearing thing) are, as a consequence, not identical.

In addition to this, we know, by inner perception, what Brentano calls the unity of consciousness (see Chapter 2, section 8: "Classification of Psychical Phenomena"). It is directly evident for us that there is a seeing thing when we are seeing, and it is directly evident for us that there is a hearing thing when we are hearing, and it is directly evident for us that there is someone who is a seeing thing and someone who is a hearing thing. Why is this someone not one of these accidents (the seeing thing or the hearing thing or a bundle of both)? Brentano argues that this someone is not one of these two accidents because either of these two accidents can fall away —as Brentano

Metaphysics

puts it— while the someone continues to exist. Here, we have a clear case showing the relation between accidents and substance. These two accidents are not identical with this someone, but this someone is the substance of these two accidents.

One of the most interesting points in Brentano's theory of accidents is that the relation between a substance and an accident is the relation of "being part of" or "being a constituent of" and not the relation of inherence of the accident in the substance as has been a tradition since Aristotle introduced the concept of accident. Brentano claims that *the subject of an accident is a part or constituent of the accident.* For example, the hearing thing is an accident, the substance is part of this accident:

Accident = The whole *hearing thing*
Substance= The mere *thing*

In other words, the substance is part of the accident; so an accident cannot inhere in a substance. This is an important departure from the Aristotelian tradition and an interesting originality of Brentano. In this way, Brentano thinks he can avoid talking about abstract entities such as red, hearing, etc., instead he talks about red things, hearing things, etc. An accident without a subject is both metaphysically an impossible and an abstract term with no real meaning.

Let us see this from the point of view of linguistic analysis. Brentano says that the accident is a thing other than the substance, but paradoxically each is predicated of the other. This means that a substance is not defined by being the subject of a predication.[13]

• First case, if the substance is predicated of an accident, then the predication asserts, not that the substance and accident are identical, but that the accident contains the substance. For example, "wise is Socrates" is like saying "the thing that is wise is the thing that is Socrates," where the accident wise contains the substance.

• Second case, if the accident is predicated of the substance, then the predication asserts that the substance is contained in the accident. For example, "Socrates is wise" is like saying "the thing that is Socrates is the thing that is wise," where the substance Socrates is contained in the accident wise (the thing that is wise).

From here we can see that the accident is a whole which has the subject as one of its proper parts. Nevertheless, although the subject is a proper part of an accident, the opposite is not correct because the accident does not contain any other proper part in addition to the subject. If the subject has proper parts; hence, then every proper part of the subject is a proper part of the accident as well. In conclusion, the proper part of the accident is the subject or a proper part of the subject. Let us see an example. The accident hearer has as its proper part the person, who is the subject of the accident hearer. This accident is detachable in the sense that the person can survive if the hearer ceases to hear, but not in the sense that the accident hearer can exist by itself without a subject. In summary, Brentano's reism in the doctrine of accidents states that there are no judgments, runs, and whites, but only judgers, runners and white things, that is to say, there are no abstract qualities or abstract entities but subjects (things) which have these qualities.

Let me insist on the reason of this view of an accident: Brentano's reism. Everything that exists is an *individual concrete*, a real thing. Now, according to Aristotle, accidents are additions to things, for example, the quality green to a plant. Now, what kind of reality is a quality? A quality that is detached from its subject is a purely and simply abstract (abstract means separated from). Brentano does not accept abstracts and universals, he only accepts individual and concrete things. Brentano solves this problem by modifying Aristotle's theory of substance and accident: it is not the accident that is attached to a substance but the substance that is included within the accident as a proper part. In other words, Brentano conceives of the accident not as an extra entity existing alongside the substance, there are no such qualities because abstracts are not individual things, instead we have qualified things. Brentano conceives of an accident as the substance itself augmented modally: *the accident is a modal extension of the substance*. This conception of accident seems to be influenced by Brentano's readings of the Spanish philosopher Francisco Suárez (1548-1617), who developed a modal theory of being in his *Metaphysical Disputations*.

Brentano agrees with the Aristotelian conception of accident as a being which requires another being as its subject, but with important differences. For Aristotle, an accident exists in (inheres in) a subject, and he does not mention that the subject is a part of the accident, but that the accident and the subject are two beings that form the whole. For Brentano, an accident is a whole which requires its subject as a part, and a whole has its parts necessarily (otherwise, it would not be a whole); from here, we have that the accident cannot exist unless its subject is a being existing in the mode of present. But there is a sense in which Brentano and Aristotle say the same thing. For both thinkers the *concept* of accident contains the substance. The substance cannot be omitted in the definition of the accident, at least in a vague and general mode.[14] But this is different than to say that the accident is a whole whose proper part is the substance.

As we know, the main source of empirical knowledge for Brentano is inner perception, and by means of inner perception we know that there are things that are accidents of other things (i.e., the

Metaphysics

hearer is an accident of myself), and by means of inner perception we also know that there are *accidents of accidents*. It is evident in inner perception that it is not possible to judge something without previously presenting this something. From here, Brentano draws the conclusion that the judging thing is an accident of the presenting thing, and this, in turn, is an accident of the substance which is the person or self.[15] We can have the experience of presentation without having the experience of judging, but we cannot have the experience of judging without having the experience of presentation. We have here the accident judger of the accident presenter. (According to Brentano, Aristotle missed this important fact about accidents, but many Aristotelians will contest Brentano on this point. Aristotle seemed to maintain that some sense qualities such as a color are accidents of the material substance through the accident extension.)

If we apply the metaphysics of accident to the mind, we have the following picture. A psychical act is an accident. When I have a psychical act, the subject of this act is present as a part of the act. The act is not some extra entity attached to the self just as an accident is not an extra entity added to the substance. It is the self —as the substance of my psychical acts— *augmenting itself* while I am having the mental activity. In this way, the self is playing the role of a part of that whole which is its accident psychical act (in other words, a psychical act is not something detached, but it is the subject performing that psychical act). This application of the metaphysics of accidents explains how the self is present to me when I am having an experience of any kind. For example, the act of seeing is an accident which has the self as its proper part (to avoid confusion, the use of the term "see-er" is clearer and suitable to Brentano's ideas than the term "act of seeing," which suggests a thing detachable from the subject; nevertheless, I will use both terms interchangeably); so, having the psychical act of seeing is at the same time having the presence of the self as its subject. In other words, being a see-er (the seeing thing) implies that the proper part is the self. This account is another explanation for the unity of consciousness: psychical experience is not resolved into a multiplicity of separate experiences, but each psychical experience contains the self as its subject. In other words, there is an element or nucleus that is constant and common to all our psychical experience diachronically and synchronically.

5. Metaphysics of Substance

In Brentano's view, a substance is better understood in relation to the accident;[16] therefore, what we gained from the study of an accident has to be applied to the study of a substance. According to Aristotle a

Metaphysics

substance is defined essentially as the bearer of accidents. Brentano contests this Aristotelian conception of substance, a conception that he accepts but with important modifications:

(1) Substances are not the only things that have accidents, as we saw in the last section, there are accidents of accidents.

(2) Brentano contemplates the possibility that there are substances that do not have accidents at all, something that Aristotle did not mention except in the case of God.

Based on these two observations, Brentano concludes that a better definition of substance is not as the bearer of accidents but the following: *a substance is a being that cannot be an accident.* However, this is not exact either because boundaries are neither substance nor accidents. For example, continuous extended things contain boundaries (surfaces, lines, or points). But because boundaries cannot be the bearer of accidents, we can modify Brentano's definition of substance slightly in the following way: *a substance is a being that cannot be an accident but is capable of having accidents.*[17]

The relation between substance and accidents is that of *one-sided separability*. Consider an aggregate of stones. Each stone can be separated from the rest, and both will survive. Here the stones in the aggregate of stones are mutually separable from each other. Each is independent of the others because it does not need the others to exist. Now, consider a red stone. If the stone is the substance and the quality red the accident, then the quality red is inseparable from the surface of the stone (there is no existing redness walking on the street), but the substance stone can be separated from the color red to acquire another color, or no color at all (black), and at the same time survive the separation. This shows that substance is separable from its accidents, but accidents cannot be separated from their substance (they will vanish). The idea of a subsisting accident would be absurd just as the idea of "modally extended" (which is the description of accident given above) without the substance that is modally extended. There is nothing left over once the substance is destroyed.

How can we prove that there are substances? We know by inner perception that accidents exist, but it seems dubious that we can perceive the existence of substance after Hume's criticism of the theory of substance. As we know so far, an accident needs a bearer, but this bearer does not have to be a substance, it can be another accident. So, maybe there is an infinite series of accidents of accidents and no substance in the end.

In Brentano's metaphysics an infinite series of accidents of accidents is not possible because the whole series would be like an accident, which by definition of the concept of accident, necessarily requires a substance as its proper part. So, if there is an accident, then there is an ultimate subsisting part or substance. From here, Brentano proposes another definition of substance that is complementary of the above definition: *substance is the ultimate subsisting part that subsists without containing any part that subsists.*[18]

We can better illustrate Brentano's idea of substance in its application to God. Brentano says that in a sense, God cannot be a substance because God *is not capable* of having accidents: God's thinking is not an accident in him, God's thinking and the being of God are identical (God cannot cease thinking). But substance is not only the ultimate bearer of accidents, it is the principle that individuates accidents.[19] An accident becomes individuated as being an accident of this substance. So, a substance is something subsisting and individuating. Given the last account, it is possible to say of God that he is a substance[20] in the sense that God is subsisting and individual, or as Brentano puts it, God is the *primary individual or primary being.*

A primary individual is the essence of being a substance. A primary individual is a being that subsists in itself. An accident, on the contrary, is something that has to exist in another thing, it is not subsisting. Boundaries do not exist by themselves, they are *part* of a continuum, but they are not accidents. A point exists only as a part of a line, and a line exists only as a part of a surface, and a surface exists only as a part of a body: *boundaries are things that need to be parts.* So, boundaries are not subsisting beings, they are parts of a whole without being accidents. On the contrary, something exists in itself —subsists— if it does *not need* to have parts and it does *not need* to be a part. And this is the primary individual, a notion that can be attributed to God, who does not have parts and is not a part of anything.

One can notice easily that the aforementioned examples of accidents and substance given by Brentano are psychical phenomena and persons respectively. A person is the substance and the mental acts are the accidents of this substance. This is a consequence of the very method that Brentano uses: empirical knowledge by inner perception. Now, are there other substances and accidents in Brentano's metaphysics? Can we talk about substances and accidents based in the external perception? Brentano cannot say with evidence the final nature of our physical world. Brentano suggests that physical bodies may be primary individuals without accidents, or may be a plurality of substances with accidents. What seems to be clear for him is that bodies are not accidents. It remains that bodies are subjects (substances) of accidents or primary individuals (subsisting things without accidents). The latter is a possibility as far as bodies do not have mental activity, which are accidents of a person (again, Brentano has as the model of his meta-

Metaphysics

physics what is perceived internally).[21]　In addition to this, bodies have parts, which are separable reciprocally, and in this sense they behave as substances. Brentano suggests a third possibility, namely, the possibility that the totality of what is corporeal may be a single bodily substance, and that the physical bodies studied by natural sciences are parts of the single substance with accidents that are the properties.

6. Metaphysics of Relation: the Intentional Relation

Brentano's theory of relation is closely connected to the relation of intentionality. Because of this, we will treat both under the same section. The theory of relation and intentional relation presented here is the last development of Brentano's philosophy. It differs qualitatively from the theory presented in his *Psychology from an Empirical Point of View* (see Chapter 2 here).

A relation is a kind of accident, so most of what we know about an accident in general must be applied to the notion of relation. In addition to this, a relation has some new features a regular accident lacks. A relation is defined by an ordered pair of things. The first is called the *foundation* of the relation, and the second the *terminus*. However, the relation is neither the foundation nor the terminus but a third element which is an accident of a substance. The foundation of a relation is presented to our consciousness *in modo recto*, that is to say, we know the foundation directly when a relation is present; and the terminus is presented *in modo obliquo*, that is, we know the terminus concomitantly when the relation and its foundation are presented. The foundation of a relation is in the subject of the relation, and in this sense, the relation is an accident. The foundation is both what generates the relation and what lies in the subject. The terminus of a relation is the reference of the relation, but the terminus is not the subject of the relation. Thus, a relation is not supported by two things (foundation and terminus) but only by the subject which is on the side of the foundation. A characteristic of a relation is that both the foundation and the terminus are real individual things. For example, in the relation "bigger than," the foundation and terminus are real things. Socrates is bigger than Plato is a real relation because really Socrates (who is a real individual) is bigger than Plato (who is another real individual), otherwise the expression "Socrates is bigger than Plato" would be false. The foundation of this relation is in Socrates, who is the subject of the relation, and the terminus is Plato. The relation as an accident has as its proper part the subject Socrates and not Plato, who is only the terminus of reference. Other examples of relation given by Brentano are the relations of smaller than, equality and iden-

Metaphysics

tity relations, cause and effect relations, etc. Some are static relations such as relations of quantity (bigger than, smaller than, etc.); others are dynamic relations such as cause/effect, etc.

This theory of relation is almost identical to Aristotle's. But Brentano in his reistic period claims an important departure from Aristotle: there are real relations in which the terminus does not exist. This special relation is the relation of intentionality. When someone thinks of an object, only the thinker necessarily exists, not the object of his thought. The nature of the relation of intentionality is very particular, and Brentano called it "quasi-relation," something relative that does not fulfill the whole definition of a regular relation. According to this period of Brentano's philosophy, psychical acts are essentially relative; they are real relations in which the foundations exist while the terminus does not have to exist. Somebody familiar with Fodor's propositional attitudes and his Language of Thought Hypothesis will discover that both philosophers —Brentano and Fodor— maintain the idea that mental acts (in Fodor, some mental acts such as propositional attitudes) are essentially relative, a relation to an object.

In a relation of intentionality, as in a regular relation, the terminus is presented *in modo recto*, and the foundation *in modo obliquo*. Brentano applies this to the relation of intentionality. We know our own subject only concomitantly while we are knowing the object of knowledge, that is to say, the relation of intentionality refers directly to the terminus, which is an object that does not have to exist, and incidentally the foundation of the relation, the psychical act of thinking, which is, in turn, an accident of the self.

Now, in Brentano's reistic period, the relation of intentionality undergoes other important modifications. Certainly, a characteristic of any psychical act is that it stands in relation to something as an object, but this object possesses only a *synsemantic* value, that is to say, the immanence of the intentional object, or the intentional inexistence, is a mere synsemantic correlate of the mental act. This has to be in this way because there is no realism for universals and ideal objects, only being in the strict sense is real, concrete and individual.

With the explicit reism of 1911, the relation of intentionality has the following characteristics: (a) When one affirms an intentional object (the Centaur, Aladdin Lamp, etc.), what one affirms is *in modo recto* (directly) the activity of the subject presenting or judging something. (b) This something has only an indirect function inasmuch as somebody presents or judges it, but *this something in itself is not the object of an affirmation at all*. The thinking subject is the only necessary condition for the relation of intentionality. The change in Brentano's theory of intentionality is important because it is no longer necessary

75

Metaphysics

to accept intentional objects as such. The singularity of the relation of intentionality is that it only requires the existence of the foundation of the relation, but the existence of the terminus is not necessary; so, Brentano is not committed to the acceptance of the terminus as an intentional object with intentional inexistence. This has as a result that *all psychical acts (all conscious acts) are essentially relative*. The nature of a psychical act is a special relation where only the foundation is necessary. The terminus of a relation of intentionality is a neutral object (existential neutrality), which can or can not exist.

If we take into consideration the accidental character of a relation, we can understand Brentano's statement that thinking is an enrichment of the subject, a *modal extension* of the subject. This is just the application of the general characteristics of an accident to the accident relation. All accidents are an enrichment of the subject, an extension of the reality of the subject.

It is interesting to see, that the consequence of rejecting ideal objects as objects is that what is the first known is the very subject and not the object. This is a sophistication of Descartes' foundationalism in which we start our knowledge from the privileged access to our subject. The question is whether the first known is really the subject and not the object in the world. When Brentano wrote his *Psychology from an Empirical Point of View*, he maintained that the physical object is first known, and the psychical phenomenon is incidentally known while we are knowing the physical object. After 1911, in his reistic period, Brentano's foundationalism inverts the terms, and the affirmation of the existence of the subject plays the main role.

We can summarize in three axioms some ideas developed so far in which Brentano's philosophy operates: (a) Inner perception is the beginning of our knowledge and provides us with immediate evidence; (b) There are only individual things, which are the only objects of knowledge; and (c) existential judgments do not have a predicative structure.

7. Metaphysics of God

The study of God is part of metaphysics, perhaps the last chapter of an Aristotelian metaphysics, and Brentano conceives of the study of God as the pinnacle of metaphysics. Brentano is well known for his psychological investigations, but his study of God is almost unknown among contemporary philosophers. Nevertheless, Brentano dedicated a good number of lectures and correspondence with many original arguments and insights to this topic. Brentano's disciple Alfred Kastil put all this material together under the title *"The Existence of God,"* a posthumous work.[22] In this section I will focus only in a few topics

Metaphysics

of interest.

As in the rest of Brentano's philosophy, the method of his metaphysics of God is the same as the method of the natural sciences, namely, it starts from experience. This is important to stress now because Brentano's arguments are directed to those philosophers who think that in a future day science will replace God. Brentano wants to provide new grounds to show that the very method of natural science is enough to prove the existence and nature of God. Brentano uses a tremendous amount of scientific data, scientific experience, and scientific theories of his time, and puts them together to forge arguments that support the existence of God.

According to Brentano, the certainty of a possible proof of God's existence is physical and not mathematical. There is no mathematical certainty of God's existence, there is no *a priori* proof of God's existence, only *a posteriori*, which provides only a physical certainty. Brentano knows Laplace's theory of probabilities very well, and uses it to say that a physical certainty of God's existence means that the certainty is not absolute, but it has a probability of infinite value.[23] This is the same case as the existence of the external world, and some data from memory. We do not have an absolute certainty of them, but they enjoy the maximal probability.

Brentano has an interesting critique of the ontological argument. This argument says: God is infinitely prefect, what is infinitely perfect has all perfections; existence is a perfection; therefore, God has to exist. One of Brentano's objections is that there is in the ontological argument a confusion of a negative judgment with an affirmative judgment. For example, consider the principle of identity "A is A" which is evident *a priori*. An instantiation of this principle is, for instance, "a man is a man". But "a man is a man" is equivalent to "there is a man who is a man," and this is equivalent to "there is a man". Now, "a man is a man" is indeed evident *a priori*, but "there is a man" is not evident *a priori* at all. The problem, so Brentano claims, is that one is taking the negative judgment as an affirmative one. The judgment "a man is a man" is in reality a negative judgment (as we saw in Chapter 3: "Theory of Knowledge") of the type: "there is no man who is not a man". And this is indeed evident *a priori*, otherwise, it will be a contradiction. Mathematical judgments belong to this kind of judgments which are *affirmative in appearance but of negative meaning*. The judgment "a square has four sides" is *a priori*, but it does not affirm that there are squares that have four sides, but that "there are no squares, which do not have four sides." Thus, Brentano avoids any commitment to existence. This has the interesting conclusion that what belongs to a concept of something cannot be said positively of it

Metaphysics

a priori but only in a hypothetical way. It is not correct to affirm *a priori* and positively that a property belongs to the subject but only negatively. This is what happens with the ontological argument. That God posses all perfections does not mean that God exists, but only that "there is no God, who does not have that existence." There is no commitment with God's existence, which still has to be proved.[24]

Brentano dedicates to the teleological argument many more pages than the combination of the other proofs taken together. It seems as if Brentano would have written these lectures for the teleological argument. Brentano's arguments are a sophistication of the classical teleological argument (the order of the universe requires an ordering cause, which is an ordering intellect). All Brentano's arguments start with the same structure: analysis of a purpose in the physical data; things are so ordered to each other that an intelligence is required as the cause of this order or purpose. Perhaps, it is interesting to say that Brentano supports the theory of evolution as a scientific theory which implies teleology, but he rejects Darwin's evolutionary explanation. Brentano is an evolutionist but not a Darwinist. He considers Darwin's natural selection not scientifically proven and very improbable, and he shows this with enough scientific data from the science of his time. Brentano sees in the evolution of biological species a teleological process that can be used to prove God's existence. The order and sense of evolution requires an ordering cause, an intelligence.[25]

Brentano conceives of God as a perfect being, creator, and infinite intelligence, transcendent, necessary, etc., but surprisingly, Brentano thinks that God is not immutable. The following is an outline of his argument. To begin with, Brentano does not use the affirmative judgment, he says that "There is no God, who is absolutely immutable." God is mutable; he changes, in order to be faithful to himself. Once said, if God created this universe, and in general if there is an x that did not always exist, then it is necessary that the cause of the universe, or the cause of this x, really becomes a cause. But if God caused the existence of the universe at a certain time, then God was not a cause before that time. Therefore, God underwent a change to produce the universe, and in general to produce any x that did not always exist.[26] One could say, that in this Brentanian argument, God behaves as a modern politician: he changes in order to be faithful to himself. God needs to change in order to create and intervene in any event of the world because to *become* a cause is a type of change.

Endnotes

[1] Carl Stumpf, "Reminiscences of Franz Brentano," in *The*

Metaphysics

Philosophy of Brentano, p. 16.
2 Cf. Brentano, *Lectures on Metaphysics*, manuscript B16499 of Brentano Archiv, in Forsschungstelle für Österreiche philosophie Dokumentationszentrum, Austria, Graz.
3 Cf. Franz Brentano, *On the Several Senses of Being in Aristotle*, translated and edited by Rolf George, Berkeley, University of California Press, 1975, p. 4.
4 Cf. Brentano, *On the Several Senses of Being in Aristotle*, pp. 15-26.
5 Cf. Brentano, *On the Several Senses of Being in Aristotle*, pp. 75ff.
6 Brentano, *On the Several Senses of Being in Aristotle*, p. 76.
7 Brentano, *On the Several Senses of Being in Aristotle*, p. 86ff.
8 Cf. Tadeusz Kotarbinski, "Franz Brentano as Reist," in *The Philosophy of Brentano*, pp. 194-203.
9 Cf. Brentano, *Psychology*, pp. 333-334.
10 Cf. Brentano, *The True and the Evident*, p. 108.
11 Cf. Franz Brentano, *The Theory of Categories*, translated by Roderick Chisholm and Norbert Guterman, Martinus Nijhoff Publishers, The Hague, 1981, pp. 15-23.
12 Cf. Brentano, *The Theory of Categories*, p. 19.
13 Cf. Brentano, *The Theory of Categories*, p.20.
14 Cf. Brentano, *The Theory if Categories*, p. 81.
15 Cf. Brentano, *The Theory of Categories*, p.86.
16 Cf. Brentano, *The Theory of Categories*, p. 111.
17 Cf. Roderick Chisholm, "Introduction to the Theory of Categories" in Brentano, *Theory of Categories*, p.9.
18 Cf. Brentano, *The Theory of Categories*, p. 114.
19 Cf. Brentano, *The Theory of Categories*, pp. 26-27.
20 Cf. Brentano, *The Theory of Categories*, p. 115.
21 Cf. Brentano, *The Theory of Categories*, pp. 209-211.
22 Cf. Franz Brentano, *Vom Dasein Gottes*, ed. Alfred Kastil, Verlag Felix Meiner, Hamburg, 1929. There is no English translation yet, and to my knowledge there is only a Spanish translation, *Sobre la Existencia de Dios*, tr. Antonio Millán-Puelles, Rialp, Madrid, 1979.
23 Brentano, *Vom Dasein Gottes*, n. 150.
24 Cf. Brentano, *Vom Dasein Gottes*, nn. 39, 42, 43.
25 Cf. Brentano, *Vom Dasein Gottes*, nn. 305 ff.
26 Cf. Brentano, *Vom Dasein Gottes*, "Logical way to prove God's Existence" nn.17-19.

5
Ethics

1. The Scope of Ethics

Brentano's ethical theory is found mainly in two works: *The Origin of our Knowledge of Right and Wrong*[1] and in the posthumous book *The Foundation and Construction of Ethics*[2]. Brentano, as before him Aristotle, conceives of ethics as the practical discipline which teaches us about the highest ends and the choice of the means for achieving the highest ends.[3] Some of Brentano's ethics is taken from utilitarianism, but his theoretical ethics (the foundation of ethics), which is Brentano's main interest in ethics, is highly original. Here, Brentano is seeking universal and self-evident ethical principles from which moral judgments can be derived.

Here, we will look at three topics: the freedom of will, the basic principle of ethics, and the concept of intrinsic good.

2. The Freedom of the Will

Brentano treats the question of the freedom of the will as a part of ethics and not as a precondition of ethics. Only acts which are able to be called morally good or bad are those which are caused by a free choice. This assumes that choice is free when it is the product of rational deliberation. Without deliberation and its product, choice, there is no sense in formulating any moral rule about what a person should do because all the acts of this person would be amoral, that is to say, without a moral qualification. Brentano thinks that the latter is not the case as a matter of fact. That we are endowed with free acts is only a matter of fact, experienced by inner perception, and not by demonstration.

Brentano distinguishes (1) the act of will itself from (2) the effect or consequence we desire it to bring about. These two concepts of freedom are frequently confused. The former is a mental activity, and the latter can be both a mental activity or a physical activity.[4] For example, to move my arm to help someone is the physical effect of a

Ethics

free act of will. We can say that the movement of my arm enjoys freedom, but freedom is in reality a property of the act of my will. The mental and physical effects of a free act of will have limits; we do not enjoy absolute freedom. Sometimes our emotions are difficult to control, and physical circumstances are serious obstacles to perform an activity. Very often, it is morally impossible to control a mental or physical act because they are under compulsion. One of the practical tasks of ethics is to master ourselves, to control our mental acts.

On the contrary, an act of free will cannot be under compulsion. Brentano thinks that freedom in the first sense (1) is a fact of experience and it is always in our power. On the contrary, our action (freedom in the second sense (2)) may be subject to coercion, but, strictly speaking, we cannot be compelled to will anything (freedom in the first sense (1)): it would be willing against our will, which is a contradiction in terms. Freedom of will is self-determination; if the act of will is compelled to act in some direction, there will no longer be self-determination, and as a result, no freedom. This is not to say that external circumstances (emotions, education, physical factors, etc.) do not influence us; it is simply a question of degree: our freedom of self-determination can decrease when we are under a strong influence of emotions, or physical constraints, etc.,[5] but if there is freedom, there is self-determination, and if there is self-determination, there is no coercion in that which there is freedom.

3. The Basic Ethical Principle

As a complement to the aforementioned definition of ethics, Brentano conceives of ethics as a discipline concerned with the first principles of action just as metaphysics is concerned with the first principles of being, and physics with the first principles of material things. The objective of Brentano's ethics is to establish the basic ethical principle or principles upon which all ethical reasoning rests.[6] Consistent with his theory of knowledge, Brentano claims that the basic moral principle has to be a directly evident judgment, implying concepts which have been acquired through inner perception of the psychical phenomena of *correct* emotions or feelings *known to be correct*. Obviously, this Brentanian position is against the idea that there are no universally and objectively valid principles of ethical knowledge.

Ethics theory just as any other theory in every area of scientific investigation such as mathematics, physics, logic, etc., is a body of judgments that has some basic principles as the foundation, from which the rest of judgments are justified or demonstrated. But these basic principles do not admit a demonstration because they do not require one. On the contrary, if everything requires a demonstration or

Ethics

proof, the process of demonstration would be a process *ad infinitum*, and as a consequence, there could be no such thing as proving something. If the series of proofs or demonstration has to end, the end is called a basic principle. This basic principle has to be evident in itself or directly evident. This means that we must have direct insight into the truth of the principle without having to learn its truth indirectly through a demonstration. Given the indemonstrability of a basic principle, is it unjustified? Not at all, this principle is self-justifying and the origin of further justifications. In this sense, Brentano is a sort of ethical intuitionist as far as we have direct insight or evidence of this basic principle. Remember, that for Brentano, when we know a directly evident judgment, we know that it is evident, otherwise, it couldn't be *directly evident*. (Most of the foundationalism in analytic philosophy is borrowed from Brentano through Chisholm, who was influenced by Brentano's theory of directly evident judgments.)

Brentano provides two criteria for basic moral principles. The first was already given, direct evidence, and the second is specific for ethics: *the effectiveness criterion*. The latter says that a basic moral principle must really lead to ethical consequences.[7] Brentano added the second criterion in objection to Kant's formal categorical imperative, which we will not discuss here.

In opposition to Hume, Brentano thinks that the basic moral principle is a type of knowledge rather than a feeling.[8] Although ethics belongs to attitudes, behavior, comportment, and feelings, it is nonetheless true that we make ethical *judgments*. For example, we say "it is wrong to lie;" which is a judgment, and as such it can be true or false, which belongs to the field of knowledge. Now, this does not mean that we can derive a judgment from a feeling or vice versa, a feeling from a judgment. Feelings, emotions and acts of will, are irreducible types of psychical acts (as we saw in the classification of mental acts, Chapter 2, last section). The reason behind Brentano's ethical intellectualism is that ethics is a rational activity, universal and valid for all rational beings, even for God. But this is not possible if ethics is based only on feelings, which depend on specific and even individual natures; so, they are not universal. Rationality is something that belongs mainly to knowledge and not to feelings.[9] Feelings are rational by derivation from being part of a correct judgment.

Now, that feelings and judgments are different categories of mental activity does not mean that feelings do not have anything to do with moral judgments. Feelings are part of moral judgments, but feelings themselves are not the basic principle. Even more, feelings are the precondition for the knowledge which constitutes the basic moral principle, but, again, they are not the basic principle. This means that

Ethics

feelings might be the objects of the moral judgment; in other words, the basic moral principle is a judgment about feelings, but feelings are not the basic principle as Hume seems to suggest. Feelings, emotions and acts of will can be the material of a moral judgment, but not the judgment itself.

Now, if ethics has to do with the highest ends of action, the basic moral principle has to do with this highest goal, which Brentano also calls "the correct end for man." So, we have to analyze now the concept of the highest end of a human action. The highest end of action can be understood in three ways that are connected: a rule, a property of the object, or an act of striving for that end. The question is which one is the starting point: the rules, the object or the striving for the object. Brentano sees a problem in the starting point. In order to know the rule, I need to know the correct end first, so I can know that the rule is correct, but I do not know the correct end of human nature if I do not have the striving for it. Brentano believes that he can escape this circle by defining the correct end of human action in terms of "correct striving." But a further question rises immediately, How do I know that a certain striving for an end is the *correct* striving? If correct striving has to be known by a rule, then we find ourselves in an undesirable circle (the rule is known because of the right end, and the right end because of the correct striving.) Nevertheless, Brentano thinks that by starting with the correct striving the logical circle is broken. These are the reasons behind Brentano's claim.

(1) If we do not have direct access to the correct end, and we do not know which one is the correct striving, then moral rules are the only candidates; and these moral rules have to be given by an external will. But a natural sanction for law and morality (the correct first principle of ethics) cannot be found in the concept of a commandment or rule given by an external will. The commandment of a rule does not make it ethical. Why does the command from an external will not sanction the morality of the rule? A command coming from an external will can never constitute the moral justification of that command or rule, though the command may in fact be morally justified, but not because it comes from an external will. The reason for this is that the concept "command coming from A" is different from the concept "correct command or correct moral rule." Therefore, the fact that a command comes from a human being or a society of human beings does not make the command morally justified.

(2) Now, the correct end cannot be defined in terms of a characteristic of an object; and this is the main reason to believe that we should start from the correct striving and not from the object (correct end) or the rule. Let us see the argument. Assuming that we have access to

Ethics

the correct end, it is not clear at all that we should pursue it. For example, if the object, which is the correct end, is happiness, it is not always clear that we should pursue it, for, maybe, in pursuing it we are acting wrongly against others. In other words, Brentano's argument states that *the concept of an end or goal does not at all involve the concept of someone striving for it.*

These arguments led Brentano to suggest that the correct striving is the starting point for establishing the basic principle of ethics. What kind of striving is correct? Brentano gives several criteria. Here are the two most significant: First, this striving has to be a striving after an end that is possible to attain, or at least that is thought to be possible to attain. Second, the striving is correct if it is a striving for the best among the ends that are possible or reasonable to attain. Having these criteria in mind, Brentano formulates the basic moral principle:

(P1)   Basic moral principle: "Choose the best among the ends that are attainable."[10]

Because this principle is formulated in positive terms, it does not mean that it has to be fulfilled at every moment (it is not possible constantly to be choosing what is best among the attainable ends.) Logically it is possible constantly to be choosing what is believed to be best, but it is impossible from a practical point of view. Brentano reformulated this principle in a negative way such that it has to be fulfilled at every moment:

(P2)   Basic moral principle   "Never choose anything less than the best that is attainable."[11]

4. The Concept of Intrinsic Good

By "intrinsic good" Brentano means that which is good in itself, or good as an end and not good just as a means for something else. Because there are no innate concepts in Brentano's philosophy, the concept of good has to come from experience. We know that there are two sources of experience, inner perception, which is a directly evident judgment, and external perception, which is just a probabilistic knowledge without evidence. Brentano suggests that the concept of good is derived from inner perception, which is tantamount to saying that the concept of good is derived from the inner perception of certain psychical acts.

What reason does Brentano have to think that the concept of good is derived from inner perception? Brentano makes an interesting and insightful analogy between the concept of truth and the concept of good. We acquire the concept of truth from the inner perception of certain acts of judgment, namely, directly evident judgments (see Chapter 3 here). Brentano suggests that the concept of good may have a similar origin but in a different class of psychical phenomenon. If truth is derived from some judgments, good may be derived from the psychical acts of will and emotion (see here Chapter 2, §6 "Classification of Psychical Phenomena.")

After having made this analogy between truth and good, one can begin to discover striking insights and possibilities:

(1) We know that truth is a property of judgments and not of things; is goodness a property of desires and emotions and not of things as well? Is an object good because there is a correct striving for that object, or the striving is correct because is directed to an object that is good? In the Aristotelian and Cartesian periods of Brentano, he thought that goodness is a property of objects. Only in the last period of his philosophy (the linguistic or reistic period) Brentano understood this analogy in a strong sense: goodness is a property of emotions, desires, and acts of will. In this section, we will not examine this idea, and we will remain with the first and second period of Brentano's ethics.

(2) Both classes of psychical acts contain opposing types of intentional relations. A judgment can be either an affirmation or a denial. Parallelly, there are opposing emotions: inclinations and disinclinations, love and hate, etc.

(3) The analogy between judgment and emotion cannot be extended to the other type of psychical phenomenon (presentations). Presentations do not have these opposing types of intentional relations. I can have the idea of green, but there are no opposing manners of referring intentionally to green as it is found in judgments and feelings.[12]

Now, with these analogies in mind, How does Brentano define the concept of good? Aristotle defined good as what is loved or what is lovable. Brentano disagreed with this because one and the same thing can be the object of opposing feelings (loved and hated), but the same thing cannot be both good in itself and bad in itself. Therefore, good cannot be defined as what is loved.

The most interesting analogy is in relation to the emotion that is correct:

(4) There is a correct and incorrect way of judging. We do not call something true just because it is affirmed, but rather when it is correctly affirmed. There is a similar opposition of intentional relations in the class of acts of will and emotions. Based on this analogy Brentano suggests that acts of will and emotions may be correct and

incorrect. In other words, the love for something which is intrinsically good is a correct emotion just as the affirmation of something which is true is a correct judgment.

Based on these analogies, Brentano provides a definition of what is "intrinsically good":

(P3) Intrinsically good: "The good is that which is worthy of love, that which can be loved with a love that is correct."[13]

Here is Brentano's equation between truth and good:

$$\frac{\text{True}}{\text{Good}} = \frac{\text{When the affirmation relating to it is correct}}{\text{When the love relating to it is correct}}$$

This analogy between a correct judgment and a correct emotion does not mean that the term "correct" is the same in both psychical phenomena. If the term was the same, then ethics would be a branch of logic, something that Brentano rejects and experience confirms. Brentano establishes the following distinctions: (a) A judgment has to do with the existence or non-existence of the objects judged. (b) Acts of will and emotions have to do with the value of their objects, and the value of an object is independent of the existence of the object. So, the two types of objects are irreducible, which is the justification to say that the two experiences are irreducible (Brentano classifies the psychical acts according to their objects.)

The analogy between correct judgment and correct love allows us to derive some axioms of correct love. We have similar laws in ethics as in logic, for example, the law of contradiction and the law of the excluded middle. These axioms of ethics are known upon experiencing the psychical phenomenon of love, which is appreciated to be correct. Let us see these axioms:[14]

(1) The existence of an object that is both correctly loved and correctly hated is impossible. (This axiom is analogous to the law of contradiction.)

(2) The existence of an object that is both incorrectly loved and incorrectly hated is impossible. (This axiom is analogous to the law of the excluded middle.)

(3) Any object capable of being loved or hated is such that either it is correct to love it or it is correct to hate it. (The Brentanian scholar, Roderick Chisholm,[15] added this principle as a natural consequence of (2).)

Ethics

How do we know that a love is correct? We know it based on the analogy between emotions and judgments. We know (see Chapter 3 here, The Theory of Knowledge) that there are true judgments; we know they are true because their truth or correctness manifests itself to us. Other judgments are true but blind, because we do not have any experience of their evidence (directly or indirectly). We can establish a similar parallelism with emotions. We can know that a love is correct if its correctness is manifested to us. To know that a love is correct is similar to how we know that a judgment is directly evident. And we know a judgment is directly evident through inner perception. Here we arrive to the most basic starting point of our knowledge of right and wrong. There is no demonstration, otherwise, the starting point or basic principle would not be the basic principle; so, it remains that there is only a self-manifestation of this basic principle.

The only way of communicating to someone what a correct love is, is by giving instantiations, examples, which can recreate the same experience in other people. Examples of correct emotions given by Brentano are pleasure in the clarity of insight, the feeling of displeasure by error and ignorance, etc. Certainly, feelings about sense quality are just a matter of taste, but this is not the case with emotions about insight and error. It is not a question of taste to love error and hate the truth, only the perversion of the feelings of a person can love error and hate truth. This is a perversion in comparison with the rest of the members of the species. The pleasure for truth is something that belongs to any rational being regardless its species. Why does this difference exist between feelings about sense quality, which are variable, and feelings about error and truth, which are universal? In the first case, feelings about sense quality depend on biological necessities, they are instinctive, and as such, they are conditioned under biological factors. In the second case, the feeling is not subject to biological conditions, it is not a feeling for biological necessities, etc., the love of truth is a higher love that is experienced as being correct for any rational being. Truth is an object capable of being loved, and error, the privation of truth, is experienced as capable of being hated. And with a single stroke, without induction from particular cases, we see the goodness or badness.[16]

In summary, Brentano claims that the source of our concept of right love or right hate comes directly from our internal experience. And when a love is correct the object of that love is good, and vice versa, when the hate is correct, the object of that hate is bad. How do we know that a certain object is good? We know it by experiencing that the object is worthy of being loved, and we know that that object is worthy of being loved if the love for this object is correct.

Ethics

Is there a circularity in Brentano's theory of correct love? Brentano does not think so. There are two important elements to consider: (a) According to Brentano, what is intrinsically good and what is worthy of love (the correct love) are logically equivalent. (b) The concept of better is an essential part of a correct love. We will dedicate the remaining section to the discussion of Brentano's notion of better.

As Chisholm points out, "a better good" in Brentano's ethics does not mean worthy of more love than another because the expression "correct love" is not a quantitative notion, that is to say, a love is not more correct or right than another: if something is intrinsically good, then it is worthy of being loved in the highest degree.[17] This statement is important because it establishes an essential difference between utilitarians and Brentano's ethics.

Brentano understands "better" in terms of *preferability*. A good is better than another means that a good is worthy of more love than another, only if the term "more" here is not interpreted as quantity. To love a good more than another, if this love is correct, it is tantamount to saying that *one good is preferable to the other*. So, preferring is what one has to understand any time one uses the expression "more love."

Interestingly, Brentano was keeping, so far, a strong analogy between both psychical phenomena —judgments and emotions. With the introduction of the concept of preference, this analogy is broken. There is no such thing as "more true" or "less true". If something is true, it seems that it is just plain true. For example, if Socrates is effectively sitting, then the statement 'Socrates is sitting" is true, but not more true when we say "Socrates is thinking" if he is effectively thinking. Everything is equally true, but not everything is equally good: we know that one good is better than another because we prefer one to the other. If we put together Brentano's theory of correct love and preference, we will have the following axiom of preference:

(P4) Preference: it is correct to prefer one good for its own sake over the other.[18]

The next question is an epistemological one, How do we know that a good is correctly preferred over another? Brentano has two possible sources:[19]

(1) Inner perception: We determine which thing is preferable by immediate perception of what is good and bad.

(2) By doing a sum in which the good and the bad are given opposite signs. Here, we can find out which things are better without the need of an act of preference that is internally perceived as being correct.

Ethics

In this case, we need only to have the internal experience of the acts of love and hate, inclination and disinclination, involved in the act of preference.

We can illustrate this with some other axioms of preference:
(1) If an object is good and another is bad, then the former is preferable to the latter.
(2) If an object is good, then the presence of this object is preferable to the absence of this object.
(3) If an object is bad, then the absence of this object is preferable to the presence of this object.

In these three axioms, we do not need to derive the correct act of preference from the experience (inner perception) of the act of preference; it is enough to experience the acts involved in the preference (acts of love and hate). Nevertheless, there are cases, in which we need to derive a correct preference from the experience (inner perception) of the act of preference, for example, in cases in which one must decide which one of two intrinsically good objects is preferable. In this case, one has to experience (inner perception) the act of preference for one of these objects as being correct; otherwise, there would not be any criterion for preference in latter cases.[20]

Endnotes

[1] Cf. Franz Brentano, *The Origin of our Knowledge of Right and Wrong*, Edited by Oskar Kraus, English Edition edited by Roderick M. Chisholm, Translated by Roderich M. Chisholm and Elizabeth H. Schneewind, Routledge & Kegan Paul, New York, 1969.
[2] Cf. Franz Brentano, *The Foundation and Construction of Ethics*, Compiled from his lectures on Practical Philosophy by Franziska Mayer-Hillebrand, English Edition edited and translated by Elizabeth Hughes Schneewind, Routledge & Kegan Paul, New York, 1973.
[3] Cf. Brentano, *The Foundation and Construction of Ethics*, p. 79.
[4] Cf. Brentano, *The Foundation and Construction of Ethics*, p. 217.
[5] Cf. Brentano, *The Foundation and Construction of Ethics*, p. 221.
[6] Cf. Brentano, *The Foundation and Construction of Ethics*, p. 22.
[7] Cf. Brentano, *The Foundation and Construction of Ethics*, p. 25.ff

[8] Cf. Brentano, *The Foundation and Construction of Ethics*, p. 38-40.
[9] Cf. Brentano, *The Foundation and Construction of Ethics*, p. 55ff.
[10] Cf. Brentano, *The Origin of our Knowledge of Right and Wrong*, p. 13.
[11] Cf. Brentano, *The Origin of our Knowledge of Right and Wrong*, p. 116.
[12] Cf. Brentano, *The Origin of our Knowledge of Right and Wrong*, p. 17ff.
[13] Brentano, *The Origin of our Knowledge of Right and Wrong*, p. 18.
[14] Cf. R. M. Chisholm, *Brentano and Intrinsic Value*, Cambridge University Press, New York, 1986, p. 55.
[15] Cf. Ibidem.
[16] Cf. Brentano, *The Origin of our Knowledge of Right and Wrong*, p. 22-24.
[17] Cf. R. M. Chisholm, *Brentano and Intrinsic Value*, Cambridge University Press, New York, 1986, p. 57f.
[18] Cf. Brentano, *The Origin of our Knowledge of Right and Wrong*, p. 25.
[19] Cf. Brentano, *The Origin of our Knowledge of Right and Wrong*, p. 27.
[20] Cf. Brentano, *The Origin of our Knowledge of Right and Wrong*, p. 28-29.

Bibliography

1. Selected Bibliography of Brentano's Published Writings

1. *Psychology from an Empirical Standpoint*, trans. by A. C. Rancurello, D.B. Terrell, and Linda López McAlister, from the second edition of volumes I and II of *Psychologie vom empirishen Standpunkt* (1924), London, Routledge & Kegan Paul, 1973.
2. *The Foundation and Construction of Ethics*, trans. by E. Schneewind, from *Grundlegung und Aufbau der Ethik* (1952), London, Routledge & Kegan Paul, 1973.
3. *Versuch über die Erkenntnis*, second enlarged edition, Hamburg, Felix Meiner, 1970.
4. *The Origin of Our Knowledge of Right and Wrong,*. trans. by R. M. Chisholm and E. Schneewind, from the 3rd edition of *Vom Ursprung sittlicher Erkenntnis* (1934), London, Routledge & Kegan Paul, 1969.
5. *The True and the Evident*, Trans. by R. M. Chisholm and E. Politzer, from *Wahrheit und Evidenz* (1930), London, Routledge & Kegan Paul, 1966.
6. *Die Abkehr vom Nichtrealem*, ed. F. Mayer-Hillebrand, Bern and Munich, A. Francke, 1966.
7. *Über die Zukunft der Philosophie*, 2nd edition, Hamburg, Felix Meiner, 1968.
8. *Die vier Phasen der Philosophie*, 2nd edition, Hamburg, Felix Meiner, 1968.
9. *Geschichte der Griechischen Philosohie*, ed. F. Mayer-Hillebrand, Bern and Munich, A. Francke, 1963.
10. *Grundzüge der Ästhetik*, ed. F. Mayer-Hillebrand, Bern, A. Francke, 1959.
11. *Die Lehre vom Richtigen Urteil*, ed. F. Mayer-Hillebrand, Bern, A. Francke, 1956.
12. *Religion und Philosophie*, ed. F. Mayer-Hillebrand, Bern, A. Francke, 1954.
13. *Vom Dasein Gottes*, ed. A. Kastil, Leipzig, Felix Meiner, 1929. The only translation I know is in Spanish: *Sobre la Existencia de Dios*, trans. by A. Millán-Puelles, Madrid, Rialp, 1979.

14. *Aristotle and his World View*, trans. by Rolf George and R. M. Chisholm, from *Aristotle und seine Weltanschaung* (1911), Berkeley, University of California Press, 1978.
15. *Descriptive Psychology*, trans. by Benito Müller, from *Deskriptive psychology* (1982), London, Routledge & Kegan Paul, 1995.
16. *On the Several Senses of Being in Aristotle*, trans. by Rolf George, from *Von der mannigfachen Bedeutung des Seienden nach Aristotle* (reprint of 1960), Berkeley, University of California Press, 1975.
17. *The Psychology of Aristotle: in Particular his Doctrine of the Active Intellect*, trans. by Rolf George, from *Die Psychology des Aristoteles* (1867), Berkeley, University of California Press, 1977.
18. *Sensory and Noetic Consciousness: Psychology from an Empirical Standpoint III*, trans. by Linda L. McAlister and Margarete Schattle, from *Vom sinnlichen und noetischen Bewutsstein* (1968), London, Routledge & Kegan Paul, 1981.
19. *The Theory of Categories*, trans. by R.M. Chisholm and Norbert Guterman, from *Kategorienlehre* (1933), Boston, Martinus Nijhoff, 1981.

2. Selected Bibliography on Brentano

1. Albertazzi, Liliana; Massimo, Libardi; and Poli, Roberto (Editors), *The School of Brentano*, Boston, Kluwer Academic Publisher, 1996.
4. Bergmann, Gustav, *Realism. A Critique of Brentano and Meinong*, Madison, Milwaukee and London, 1967.
5. Bergmann, Hugo, "Brentano's Theory of Induction", in *Philosophy and Phenomenological Research*, vol.5, Issue 2 (Dec., 1944), 281-292.
6. Chisholm, Roderick M., *Brentano and Intrinsic Value*, Cambridge, Cambridge University Press, 1986.
7. Chisholm, Roderick M., *Brentano and Meinong Studies*, Humanities Press, Atlantic Highlands, 1982.
8. Chisholm, Roderick M., "Franz Brentano," in *Encyclopedia of Philosophy*, ed. Paul Edwards, New York, 1967.
9. Gilson, Lucie, *Méthode et métaphysique selon Franz Brentano*, Paris, 1955.
11. McAlister, Linda L., *The Development of Franz Brentano's Ethics*, Amsterdam, Rodopi, 1982.
13. Smith, Barry, *Austrian Philosophy, the Legacy of Franz Brentano*, Chicago, Open Court, 1994.
14. Srzednicki, Jan, *Franz Brentano's Analysis of Truth*, The Hague, 1965.